Religious education in secondary schools

Evans / Methuen Educational

First published 1971 for the Schools Council
by Evans Brothers Limited
Montague House, Russell Square, London WC1B 5BX
and Methuen Educational Limited
11 New Fetter Lane, London EC4P 4EE

Distributed in the US by Citation Press
Scholastic Magazines Inc., 50 West 44th Street
New York, NY 10036

SBN 423 44460 3

Printed in Great Britain by
Richard Clay (The Chaucer Press) Ltd
Bungay, Suffolk

Preface

This is a working paper, not a report. Its intention is to raise questions for public discussion and to invite comments from those concerned with education, and particularly religious education, in schools. We would not claim to know all the answers, but we do believe that these are some of the questions that need to be faced at the present time if the many difficulties surrounding the teaching of religion in schools are to be understood and the pattern for the future made plain.

The working paper represents the thinking of those engaged on the work of the Schools Council Project on Religious Education in Secondary Schools after the first eighteen months. The views expressed in it must not be taken to be those of the Schools Council; they represent the views of this project alone. Any resulting changes in syllabuses must be carried out in accordance with the provisions of paragraph 26 and the fifth schedule of the 1944 Education Act.

Correspondence regarding the content of the working paper should be addressed to the Deputy Director, Project on Religious Education, Cartmel College, University of Lancaster, Bailrigg, Lancaster.

Introduction: the legacy of religion in schools

The history of religious education in Britain is inseparable from the history of education itself; it is not, as is sometimes suggested, a piratical intrusion. Universal education sprang from religious education, particularly from the initiative of the Church of England National Society and the non-conformist British and Foreign Schools Society, as well as from the wide and rapid growth of the interdenominational Sunday School movement. In 1833, when Parliament first approved plans to use public funds to assist the two Societies, the state did not consider education as one of its roles, nor was there widespread secular or religious support for it to do so. There was, however, growing agitation for secular education. Leadership and support for this movement came chiefly, not from men without religion, but from Non-conformists, who saw that the distribution of public money to existing schools gave a denominational advantage to the Church of England, since the National Society was the larger of the two and in a great many parts of the country, particularly in rural areas, the parish school had a virtual monopoly. This was the first aspect of what was soon known as 'the religious difficulty' in education in this country, and it took more than a century to find an acceptable way of dealing with it.

When, in 1870, the state itself entered the field of education another aspect of 'the religious difficulty' had to be faced, namely whether any kind of religious teaching should, or could, be given in schools provided entirely from public funds. Although at that time Christianity was the dominant religion in the country, difficulties of interpretation and sharp rivalries between Christian denominations made this a very difficult subject for teachers to handle. For this reason alone some legislators were inclined to leave religion out of publicly-financed education. There was, however, a contrary argument that troubled the politicians. As W. E. Forster put it:

> Why do we not prescribe that there shall be no religious teaching? If we did so out of the religious difficulty we should have the irreligious difficulty. We want to do what the majority of parents in this country prefer, that there should be a Christian education for their children.[1]

The English people cling to the Bible and no measure will be more un-

7

popular than that which declares by Act of Parliament that the Bible shall be excluded from the school.[2]

In the event, a small place was left for religion in the 1870 Elementary Education Act; each local school board was given the responsibility of deciding whether or not religious teaching should be given in the schools under its jurisdiction. The teaching of 'any catechism or formulary which is distinctive of any particular religious denomination' was, however, prohibited by law (the famous 'Cowper–Temple clause' of the Act). The eventual pattern was set by the London School Board, then under the powerful influence of the famous scientist and avowed atheist, Professor T. H. Huxley. It decreed:

> The Bible shall be read and there shall be given such explanation and such instruction therefrom in the principles of morality and religion as are suited to the capacity of children.[3]

Most of the other school boards followed the London example; religious instruction was included in the curriculum but it was restricted to 'scripture'. Three-quarters of a century later, by the 1944 Education Act, an attempt was made to regularize the religious provision in what were now called 'county' schools, and to liberalize its content. The local option was replaced by the mandatory provision of religious education in accordance with syllabuses drawn up, or adopted, by a conference of the main parties concerned in each local authority area. The restrictive wording of the Cowper–Temple clause was, however, repeated. (The Act also made separate provision for 'voluntary' schools and safeguarded the rights of minority groups and individual parents and teachers objecting to religious teaching on grounds of conscience.)

The religious settlement of 1870 was probably the best that could be devised at the time, but this cautious provision of non-denominational Christian teaching – even with the 1944 addition of an agreed syllabus – has not been a very satisfactory way of providing for the study of religion in schools in recent decades.[4] The rapid social and educational changes of recent years compel us to face squarely many questions of which most RE teachers were hardly aware twenty-five years ago:

1 What are the educational reasons for including any subject in the curriculum?
2 Should religion have a place? If so, what place?
3 If the term 'religious education' is used, what exactly is meant, and what is not meant, by it?
4 How far should religion be taught or studied from any one religious standpoint?

5   Is there a unique contribution made by *religious* education that is not made, for example, by *social* education or *moral* education?
6   What is the difference between the task of the school in religious education and that of the church, home, synagogue, or mosque?

For one hundred years religious teaching in maintained schools has been given by an army of teachers holding very varied, and sometimes conflicting, views as to its nature, status, and purpose. Many still see it, like the London School Board of 1870, as an exercise to make children familiar with the Bible. At the other extreme many teachers have looked upon religious education in schools as an extension of the evangelistic work of the Church. This brings to the maintained schools something of the declared objective of the Church societies. The full name of the Church of England Society, for example, was 'The National Society for Promoting the Education of the Poor in the Principles of the Established Church'. The expressed aims of some of the recent 'teacher-based' CSE syllabuses show that this view is still widely shared. The North Western Board, for example, says that its aim:

> is not simply to present the Bible as a record of historical events but to bring children into an encounter with Jesus Christ . . .

Other boards imply much the same type of approach. The East Midlands Board writes:

> The theme of the syllabus is Christian discipleship. Christian discipleship may be defined as a way of life based upon faith in Jesus Christ whom God sent to be our Deliverer and through whom man can enter into a special relationship with God.

The West Yorks and Lindsey Board writes:

> This syllabus aims at presenting to young people the challenge of the personality of Christ . . .

Without going into the questions and problems raised by taking such aims for a public examination syllabus we should note that antagonism to this 'evangelizing' type of religious education has grown in recent years. Most RE teachers now seem to be developing aims which are fundamentally educational, rather than 'confessional'. Even in Scotland, where confrontation with these issues has been avoided by reference to the statutory phrase 'in accordance with use and wont', there are signs that a similar re-appraisal is taking place.[5] Our evidence suggests that fundamental questions about the place of religion in education are being asked in almost every country of the Western world, and that

9

there is a remarkable consensus of opinion as to the answers. In the USA the whole issue has been opened afresh. On 17 June 1963, the Supreme Court reaffirmed the ban on compulsory prayer and Bible readings in public (i.e. state) schools, as inappropriate in an educational institution provided by the state, and as inconsistent with the First Amendment to the Constitution. The Court went on however to indicate clearly that this should not be taken to exclude the study of religion from public schools. Mr Justice Brennan stated:

> Whether or not the Bible is involved, it would be impossible to teach meaningfully many subjects in the social sciences or the humanities without some mention of religion.

Later he added:

> Any attempt to impose rigid limits upon the mention of God or references to the Bible in the classroom would be fraught with dangers.

In a separate concurring opinion, Mr Justice Goldberg wrote:

> Neither the state nor this Court can or should ignore the significance of the fact that a vast portion of our people believe in and worship God and that many of our legal, political and personal values derive historically from religious teachings. Government must inevitably take cognizance of the existence of religion and, indeed, under certain circumstances the First Amendment may require that it do so. And it seems clear to me from the opinions in the present and past cases that the Court would recognize the propriety of . . . the teaching *about* religion, as distinguished from the teaching *of* religion, in the public schools.

Mr Justice Clark added:

> It might well be said that one's education is not complete without a study of comparative religion or the history of religion and its relationship to the advancement of civilization. It certainly may be said that the Bible is worthy of study for its literary and historical qualities. Nothing we have said here indicates that such study of the Bible or of religion, when presented objectively as part of a secular program of education, may not be effected consistent with the First Amendment.[6]

The great living religions of the East are now influencing our European situation. The mass media of communication have made us more aware of them, and the presence of adherents of other faiths in our own country is enriching and changing our national life. Education in Britain today needs to be education for world understanding and our conception of religious education must be suffi-

10

ciently comprehensive to promote this aim. This is true whether, in any given class, there are pupils of other faiths present or not.

Such rethinking of the scope and intention of religious education in schools can help in another direction. The dialogue of our day is mostly with those who have no religious faith. We are convinced that it is proper to provide all pupils with opportunities to consider religious issues and the means whereby they will understand religious beliefs and actions. We suggest, however, that there is something wrong with an aspect of the curriculum when it is expected at the outset that some parents and teachers will wish to opt out on *grounds of conscience*.

We would, therefore, ask if there is an approach to the study of religion in school which all fair-minded people can agree is a proper part of education and which will receive, in the words of the Social Morality Council:

> . . . the wholehearted support of the people of this country, because it is of prime personal and national interest, concerned with the roots and future of our society, and no less vital than technology.[7]

Part I

The main inquiry: the character of religious education

I. Why study religion in schools?

There appear to be four main arguments for the inclusion of religion in the curriculum of the maintained schools.

1 There is evidence that most parents, most teachers and, perhaps, most pupils wish it to be included.[8] The reasons for this may be complex. It may be that, as a number of opinion polls have indicated, the bulk of the population of the British Isles still claims allegiance to Christianity. The habit of church-going has declined, but masses of people who never attend church, except perhaps for baptisms, weddings, and funerals, conform to social customs with a Christian background and by their conduct and attitudes show that they are still guided largely by principles having a Christian origin.

It may be simply that the public wants for its children something more than 'virtuous materialism'. Harold Loukes interprets the intention of the parents in these terms:

> What we want . . . is that besides setting geographers to show our children geography and mathematicians to show them mathematics, you should arrange for some good people to show them goodness; not just 'being good', but the vision of goodness – something that will work on them.[9]

> Awaken our children to the largeness of the world they live in, give them a dream of human achievement and an active concern for the human predicament here and now. And if you must call them God and Christ and Spirit, well and good, but it is the awakening we ask for, not the terminology.[10]

Of school assemblies, Loukes hears them saying:

> I want you to make him think about good things, have high thoughts, share in an experience that will make him more magnanimous, give him a sense of mystery and meaning in mystery.[11]

2 The tradition of our national life has been largely shaped and sustained by behaviour and ideas closely associated with the practice of religion, and particularly the Christian religion. Since education involves a thorough exploration of the environment and the received culture, this source of our national heritage should be studied and appreciated. An investigation of religion and its claims is thus an important part of education in Britain, whether the pupils have any religious affiliation or not.

15

3 A third argument arises from the nature of religion itself. Although no single definition of religion is adequate – either the definitions are too broad and hence vague and meaningless, or they are too narrow and hence exclude some religious phenomena; still religion has to do basically with discernment and commitment.[12] Religions claim to discern the meaning and purpose of life; they also commit their adherents to action appropriate to this discernment (usually this commitment involves a community of believers, ritual for the renewal of vision and commitment, and instruments for the proclamation and carrying out of its message). In brief, and greatly over-simplified, religion is that insight for which a person gives his life. Because of the depth (discernment) and power (commitment) of religion the study of religion at a level appropriate to the pupil seems a necessity.[13]

4 The fourth argument arises from modern educational theory; that any liberal education must provide as fully as possible for the natural development of the child. Young children have a deep sense of wonder and awe. Unless this side of a child's personality is respected and developed his personality will be stunted in one direction. Similarly, a genuine search for meaning in life is characteristic of older children. They have a tremendous interest in religious phenomena and are sensitive to many of the finer and deeper aspects of human experience of which religion speaks. Education should encourage and develop this search, making the pupil aware of the questions and the concerns of religion, and giving him experience of the methods of inquiry, the language, and thought-forms that belong to this form of discourse.

Since, like history, art, mathematics, or science, religion is a distinctive way of interpreting experience, a mode of understanding, anyone who grows up not seeing and feeling that there is such a thing as genuine religious belief is, to that extent, undeveloped and incomplete as a human being.[14]

From the time of the Spens Report of 1938 this has been the recurring theme in educational charters:

> No boy or girl can be counted as properly educated unless he or she has been made aware of the fact of the existence of a religious interpretation of life. (Spens Report, 1938)[15]

> The teenagers with whom we are concerned need, perhaps above all else, to find a faith to live by. They will not find precisely the same faith and some will not find any. Education can and should play some part in the search. It can assure them that there is something to search for and it can show them where to look and what other men have found.
> (Crowther Report, 1959)[16]

The nearer we got to the boys and girls on whose education we have to advise, the more it was brought home to us that Parliament gave the schools a difficult but not impossible task when it told them to foster their spiritual and moral development. We learned that those who tried with sincerity and ability to do this found that they were not only fulfilling a statutory obligation or discharging a social responsibility; they were meeting a felt personal need of their pupils. Most boys and girls want to be what they call 'being good' and they want to know what this really implies in the personal situations which confront them. This is difficult enough but it is not sufficient. They want also to know what kind of animal a man is and whether ultimately each one of us matters – and if so why and to whom.

(Newsom Report, 1963) [17]

Valuable though these statements are they seem to us to concentrate mainly on one aspect of religious education. More recent statements of aims attempt to do justice to other aspects. They also, most significantly, indicate what they consider to be a proper educational approach to religion in schools:

We take its comprehensive purpose to be:

to help children and young people to grow up into whole and mature people, with understanding of themselves, able to develop good relations with other people and the world around them, and capable of responding to God.

For this purpose it aims

to give them a feeling for and an understanding of the religious dimension of life and its interpretation

to put them in a position to appreciate the Judaeo–Christian heritage which has played a powerful role in their culture, and to inform them about the life and teaching of Christ and the growth of the Church to modern times

to help provide them with an understanding of religious symbols and language so as to enable them to reformulate a faith for the future

to give them the experiences and opportunities through which they can face the claim of Christianity and make a free and responsible decision about it for themselves.

(Christian Education Movement and British Council of Churches) [18]

The British Council of Churches adds:

It should be clear that the aim of religious education in county schools is to deepen understanding and insight, not to proselytize. [19]

The Social Morality Council, a body which includes Catholics, Protestants, Jews, and Humanists, writes:

> The aim of religious education in a county school is to enable a boy or girl to have a proper understanding of what is meant by a religious approach to life, and for most children in this country the centre of this understanding will be the Christian approach. It is not the purpose of religious education in the county school to bring about a commitment to the Christian faith, but rather to help children to understand what the Christian faith means in the context of other beliefs sincerely held by men and women of integrity and goodwill who do not find it possible to accept a Christian commitment as the basis of their lives. One of the results of religious education should be to create in boys and girls a more sensitive understanding of their own beliefs and of the different beliefs by which others govern their lives; such a sensitive understanding is not the prerogative of Christians.[20]

The religious and cultural panel of the Birmingham Community Relations Committee includes Sikhs, Muslims, Hindus, Jews, and representatives of the main Christian churches in the area as well as of the teachers' organizations. The panel writes:

> There are at least three aspects to the common background which should be provided for all children:
>
> a It should be part of an education for life in this country that children come to know something of the traditional religion of the land, namely Christianity. There is in general no conflict of interests at this point, for it is noteworthy that Asian families, whilst holding firmly to their own faith, are usually anxious that their children should also be fully introduced to the 'British way of life', including its religious aspects;
>
> b It should be part of a general education today to become aware of the diverse forms both of human culture and of religious faith. In the field of religious education this means that children should not be ignorant (as too often they have been in the past) of the main features of the major world religions; and that in Birmingham, more specifically, Christian children should know something about the Hindu, Islamic, Judaic, and Sikh faiths which are part of our pluralistic scene, just as children of these various faiths should know something both of Christianity, as the majority faith of the country, and of the other minority faiths;
>
> c The term 'religious education' covers, in practice, the very important field of moral education about which much important research has been

done in recent years. It should be noted that this aspect of 'religious education' is of great concern to humanists, and others not committed to any of the traditional faiths, as well as to religious believers.

Thus the parts of the agreed syllabus concerned with the common background of understanding should provide education about Christianity and about at least those other major religious faiths and philosophies which are significantly represented in the community both in and outside school.

The Church of England Commission on Religious Education in Schools (the Durham Commission) writes:

> The aim of religious education should be to explore the place and significance of religion in human life and so to make a distinctive contribution to each pupil's search for a faith by which to live. To achieve this aim, the teacher will seek to introduce most pupils to that biblical, historical and theological knowledge which forms the cognitive basis of the Christian faith . . . to show his pupils the insights provided by Christian faith and experience into a wide range of personal, social and ethical problems . . . to discuss with his pupils the various answers and approaches provided by this faith to those basic questions of life and existence which perplex all thoughtful men. Where appropriate he will study other religions and belief systems. The teacher is thus seeking rather to initiate his pupils into knowledge which he encourages them to explore and appreciate, than into a system of belief which he requires them to accept. To press for acceptance of a particular faith or belief system is the duty and privilege of the Churches and other similar religious bodies. It is certainly not the task of a teacher in a county school. If the teacher is to press for any conversion, it is conversion from a shallow and unreflective attitude to life. If he is to press for commitment, it is commitment to the religious quest, to that search for meaning, purpose and value which is open to all men.[21]

There are two distinct but related fields open for exploration in the study of religion. For convenience these may be referred to as 'explicit' religion and 'implicit' religion. Explicit religion is religion as a phenomenon; implicit religion resides in those elements of secular experience – like wonder, guilt, and love – which evoke questions about life's ultimate significance, its values, meaning, and purpose.

Some educational theorists see religious education mainly in terms of the first – the study of religion as an historical, social, and psychological phenomenon, with the study of various forms of religious expression. Others see religious education mainly as promoting and assisting the personal quest for meaning and purpose. It is our view that, all the way through the school years, in ways suited to the understanding of the children, religious education must be concerned with both of these fields, and that the one reinforces and interprets the other.[22]

Since every subject in the curriculum may be perceived in ultimate perspective, from the 'implicit' point of view every subject may contribute to the development of religious awareness and religious insight. Indeed, it is sometimes urged that, if this is what really matters in religious education, there is no need for a separate subject called RE: the study of English literature, social studies, and the arts inevitably involve religious questioning. They also provide an easy, natural context for such discussion. Should not RE disappear as a separate discipline and be absorbed in these or in some combined study of the humanities?

There is much to be said for this view, and we shall return to it in a later section. Meanwhile, two things need to be said:

1 We share Professor Niblett's view that:

> Unless periods are set apart when religious education is the prime subject of concern the danger will be considerably greater that it will be no one's business to foster this mode of apprehension and that a still larger proportion of the school week will be spent in adjusting people to a society whose aims are at best a 'virtuous materialism', with technical accomplishment, including, of course, examination success, achieved en route.[23]

2 This is only one aspect of religious education. The 'implicit' requires the guidance and reinforcement of the 'explicit' – the religious experience of mankind, in the past and today, a real understanding of the phenomena called 'religious' – institutions, beliefs, ceremonies, books, and persons regarded as sacred.

II. The approach to religion in schools

Is it possible for teachers to be objective in dealing with such an emotionally charged subject as religion, or is religion an inescapably subjective type of experience and therefore incompatible with the principles governing education in maintained schools? There have been three approaches to this question.

1 *The 'confessional' or dogmatic approach*
This begins with the assumption that the aim of religious education is intellectual and cultic indoctrination. It is often linked with a belief that any other kind of religious education is valueless or unworthy of the name. This has been the traditional view of the Roman Catholic Church in this country, of some Jewish and Muslim leaders, and of some Protestants.

2 *The anti-dogmatic approach*
This rules out the subjective element from religious education and conceives it as an academic exercise, dispassionate and objective. The National Secular Society, for example, suggests that the study of religion on these terms should be included as part of the history syllabus. The report of the Committee on Religious Education in the public schools of the Province of Ontario, issued in 1969, also recommends this sort of approach.

3 *The 'phenomenological' or undogmatic approach*
This sees the aim of religious education as the promotion of understanding. It uses the tools of scholarship in order to enter into an empathic experience of the faith of individuals and groups. It does not seek to promote any one religious viewpoint but it recognizes that the study of religion must transcend the merely informative. Pioneer work on these lines has already met with success at the Universities of Lancaster and Leicester. There are, however, a great many teachers in secondary schools, dissatisfied with both the 'confessional' and the anti-dogmatic approaches, who have been working their way, almost by instinct, to this – the educational approach. This paper is intended to clarify that approach and to explore its implications.

The central issue is the meaning of *objectivity* in the study of religion and the conditions needed for its attainment.

21

Typically, every form of religion involves passionate commitment. It is a matter of what a person, or a community, regards as supremely valuable. It is not arrived at by cool detachment, but by inner recognition and personal dedication. It might appear then that any attempt to view a religious statement or activity as an object of inquiry would miss or obscure the very qualities that give it meaning as religious (i.e. as it appears in the mind and experience of the believer). If religion cannot be properly understood apart from subjectivity, then any satisfactory concept of objective study must somehow include that subjectivity. That is, the objectivity must be about the subjectivity; it must refer to ways of thinking responsibly about matters of intense personal interest and concern.

Such objectivity is actually possible because of the characteristic human capacity for self-transcendence. Human beings are not enclosed within the prison of their own subjectivity, but by the power of imagination they are able to participate in the subjectivity of others. A human being can be himself and at the same time share the life and thought of another person. A person does not react only to another person as an object. Through what is called personal communication he has the ability to perceive the other as a subject, and thus can establish a relationship of communion with him.

> This capacity for self-transcending awareness is the basis for all objective scholarship. It is not the main function of the scholar to express his own beliefs and feelings. His task is chiefly to expound and interpret the beliefs and commitments of other people. Moreover, he is obliged to do maximum justice to his subject, that is, to represent other viewpoints with insight and sympathy. He is not denied his own opportunities for advocacy and self-expression, but these activities ought not to control, colour, or interfere with his balanced and judicious treatment of positions other than his own.[24]

This human power of imaginative self-transcendence is the foundation of all scholarly objectivity and the presupposition of any intellectually responsible education. The objective study of religion is only a special case of the objective study of any subject whatsoever. There are, of course, features of religious inquiry that differentiate it from the study of other matters. Still, the same fundamental canons of sound scholarship apply in the field of religion as in other fields of investigation. Objectivity in scholarship generally and in religious matters specifically does not exclude emotions and commitments.

> It is quite feasible to study and teach objectively matters that are heavily charged with passions and interests. Such objectivity is not achieved by rising above the life of conviction into a realm of cool rational detachment. It is attained rather by the controlled deployment of one's own affective and

22

conative life in the pursuit of sympathetic understanding of the inner life of other persons. This suggests that it is persons with well-developed emotional and volitional capacities who can best identify with the deep concerns of other persons. Hence the growth of objectivity does not depend on the denial of personal commitment but on its strengthening, in order to provide the basis for awareness of commitments in others.

It is a grave misconception of scholarly endeavour and of the proper domain of public formal education to suppose that matters like religion and politics, which arouse strong and divergent feelings, cannot be handled responsibly and intelligently in public school classrooms. If they are excluded, then the basic raison d'être of critical enquiry is denied and the ideal of significant (as contrasted with trivial) objectivity is repudiated. The best climate for the cultivation of objectivity is one in which strong personal convictions are assumed and respected. Critical intelligence is fostered best in schools where studies are not regarded as exercises for the detached mind, but as opportunities for the development of responsible commitments by the whole person.

From this point of view, religion cannot be excluded from the curriculum on the ground that it is a matter of passionate interest and that the religious interests of persons in a pluralistic society are divergent. Instead, these very divergencies may be used as the basis for developing a richer and more profound objectivity. Moreover, religion, the domain of supreme commitment of the whole person, provides the best of all possible materials for the growth of this quality of objective, or critical and appreciative, intersubjective understanding.[25]

The approach to religious education should be by way of 'critical and appreciative intersubjective (or inter-personal) understanding'. It is not concerned with 'bare facts', free of all interpretative elements. In every field of study fact and interpretation belong together. Every fact is set within some framework of interpretation; every statement has some context of presuppositions. For example, the facts of physics must be understood from the standpoint of some conceptual model. They can never be conceived as absolute and invariant truths, independent of the system of assumptions and definitions into which they fit. Similarly, the facts of religion cannot be taught without presuposing some pattern of interpretative ideas.

It is often supposed, for example, that the Bible can be taught objectively in schools by presenting it as fact without interpretation. But what is meant by this presupposition? That the words of the Bible should be read without any attempt to understand their import? Such reading would be pointless. The chief point

23

in reading the Bible, or in studying any other religious entity, is to understand what it means and this calls for interpretation. Thus, any significant use of the Bible in schools inevitably involves exegesis.

Since, then, interpretation is inescapable, objectivity cannot depend on its presence or absence, but on the uses made of it. Some kinds of interpretation are incompatible with the requirements of objectivity, and others are not.

a One test of objectivity is the willingness to admit the possibility of alternative patterns of interpretation. Except where a unit of knowledge is self-evident or logically demonstrable, it must be admitted that more than one interpretation is always possible. Teaching is not objective when one interpretation is presented as though it were absolute and unquestioned fact and as though no alternative interpretations were possible or admissible.

This does not mean, and cannot mean, that the teacher must always present every possible interpretation of the topic studied. This would hopelessly overburden the teacher and confuse the pupils. Some aspects of human experience are capable of an indefinite array of such possibilities, and in many, if not most teaching situations, the teacher may be unable to present more than one interpretation. The important thing is that, whether alternative interpretations are studied or not, their possibility is not tacitly excluded. What is not defensible is any implication that interpretation is unnecessary or that a particular interpretation is the only one that may be considered.

Objective teaching seeks to present evidence for beliefs, so that they may be accepted or rejected freely and intelligently. This is why the existence of alternatives is important. Without them, the pupils enjoy no freedom of choice. Frequently, of course, one among multiple possibilities may appear overwhelmingly preferable, the evidence for it being so strong that the other options are exceedingly unattractive. Nevertheless, even in such a case the recognition of other possibilities is important to preserve the sense that belief is a free response to evidence.

In the field of religion the evidence for beliefs is usually not sufficient to raise one interpretation to the level of certainty in public debate. The matters dealt with are of great complexity and they involve the convergence and co-ordination of many lines of evidence. For this reason it is vitally important that teaching in the field of religion should give major attention to alternative systems of belief and practice.

> The purpose of academic teaching is to increase understanding, not to advocate a particular religious position. The only proper advocacy in the scholarly community is that of truth, and truth may manifestly be served

24

best by remaining open to the possibility of new and better understanding.[26]

It may be objected that such an approach may be suitable at university level, but that the average layman, and certainly young children, need a reasonably secure set of beliefs that can be accepted on authority, rather than a precarious and frequently changing system of ideas based on an awareness of possible alternatives.

Although one may have some sympathy with this point of view, the fact is that in a multi-cultural society there is no one religious (or anti-religious) position that can be taught in this way. (It is, of course, possible for a religious group to withdraw from society and to provide in its own schools religious teaching from its own point of view. There is, however, a great deal of evidence that with the spread of the mass media such 'religious' schools, including many boarding schools, are affected by public debate almost as much as the county schools; and that the untroubled and unquestioning faith of early childhood is being shaken at a very early age. Moreover, the record of human bigotry and inter-group hostility through the ages does not commend this as a national policy.)

Those who oppose the presentation of more than one religious viewpoint to young children claim that immature minds are not capable of understanding such distinctions and would only be confused. There is, of course, some merit in this claim. Young children cannot be taught in the same way as academic sixth-formers, and some developmental psychologists have demonstrated that most children are unable to cope with abstract conceptual thinking until well into the 'teens'.[27] It was for this reason, presumably, that the Plowden Report contained the much-debated sentence: 'Children should not be confused by being taught to doubt before faith is established.'[28]

Fortunately, even in the primary school, doubt and faith are not the only alternatives. It has been pointed out that in certain respects young children are even better able than older pupils to appreciate the significance of alternative perspectives.[29] Their imaginations have not yet been compromised by the demands of academic conventionality, and their thought processes have not yet been channelled into standard scholastic habits. Their world is still mostly unexplored and full of promise and they still have the capacity to envisage alternative possibilities. Junior school children, for example, are still activated by the creative spirit of play, which permits them to construct imaginative worlds that are as real as those of everyday existence. Such a spirit is of the very essence in the life of objective rationality. Prejudice and non-objective beliefs are expressions of routine and unimaginative habits of thought. One argument which has been brought against the study of religion at university level [30] is that it is too serious a matter to play with – and 'playing with ideas' is an essential part of true academic study.

The foundations for mature critical thinking are best laid in the play world of the young child. In the primary school religious understanding can be encouraged by providing for actual and imaginative participation in the life of different communities of faith. A Christian child can be a Jew for a day or an hour by witnessing a sacred festival or by acting out a part in an imagined ritual occasion. A Jewish child can identify in imagination with the Muslim community, and understand inwardly, as a loyal player in the 'game of faiths' what it means to go on pilgrimage. Objectivity is thus possible for pupils of all ages and all degrees of intellectual maturity. The same fundamental principle of self-transcending awareness governs at all intellectual levels. The difference in treatment between work with young children and that with more mature pupils is not the degree of objectivity that is possible but the degree of abstraction that can be employed in the consideration of alternative interpretations.

The main point is that in a multi-cultural society it is not the task of education to tell children which religious interpretation they should believe, but to develop in them habits of thought which will equip them to enter with understanding and sympathy into a variety of perspectives.

b But that is not enough. This openness to the possibility of alternatives is not the only condition for objectivity in religious education. Criticism is required too. It is not sufficient to parade alternatives before the eyes of the imagination and to leave it at that, as if there were no objective ways of judging their relative truth or adequacy. The special function of academic communities is to create schemes for the critical evaluation of interpretations originating in non-academic communities, whether the interest be economic, social, military, political, or religious.

Every academic discipline has developed patterns of concepts and methods to facilitate such critical comparison and appraisal. Education is thus concerned with interpreting interpretations and gaining perspective on perspectives. Although the various disciplines study different aspects of experience, they are united in a common loyalty to this principle of criticism, the search for consistency and adequacy in their interpretation of the data. That search must form an integral part of religious education in schools and, at the appropriate stages, pupils should be introduced to the methods of inquiry, and the language and the thought-forms, that are used in this kind of inquiry.

c A third pre-condition of objectivity in the study of religion is academic

26

freedom. Religious education is seen by many as the induction of the young into the beliefs and practices of a particular religious community, and its goal the perpetuation of that community. Although this process may be well suited to serve the special interests of a community of faith, it cannot be the basis for public education in a society composed of the adherents of many faiths and none.

However, this ought not to be used as an argument for the abolition of religious education and the substitution of aims based on the requirements of civil life. Secularizing the schools in this way will not ensure that the teaching in them will be more objective, since they may then be organized to propagate some approved set of civic beliefs and virtues. The systematic anti-religious propaganda efforts of the schools in the Soviet Union are a reminder that schools may just as easily be instruments of secular indoctrination as ecclesiastical. Such schools are just as fully devoted as any religious schools to the extension and perpetuation of a traditional system of belief and conviction.

Even if the civic beliefs and values are not Marxist but the 'British way of life' (whatever that is), the objection is the same. Schools should not look for their perspective either to organized religion or to the body politic, but to the insights of disciplined scholarship. That is to say, they are neither religious nor civic, but academic institutions. So far as teaching and learning are concerned, their primary loyalty is not to a traditional organized faith nor to the views of the body politic, but to the onward-going enterprise of scholars in the various fields of disciplined investigation. This is what is meant by academic freedom: the teacher is primarily responsible to the community of scholars rather than to any other social body. When this is clearly understood, a teacher will not use his position to advance any cause other than that of responsible scholarship, the pursuit of truth through the critical consideration of many viewpoints. Objective teaching of any subject in schools depends upon the existence of academic freedom, with its counterpart – the commitment of teachers to the standards of responsible scholarship.

To sum up, many writers on religious education, and many committees drafting agreed syllabuses, still assume a 'confessional' or dogmatic approach. (This is a point examined more fully in the next chapter of this working paper.) Most of the attacks on religious education in schools are criticisms of this kind of teaching. Such an approach is not only inappropriate in a multi-belief community; it is also contrary to the very spirit of education as it is understood and practised today. In every other subject children are encouraged to question and explore, to take nothing to be true until they can see it to be true. The purpose of scientific education, for example, is not to inculcate an uncritical acceptance of scientific facts, but rather to initiate pupils into the spirit of inquiry and discovery which makes science a dynamic living process. A subject which pre-

27

sumes to lay down, however subtly, what is to be believed, is noticeably out of place in schools today. It may succeed in 'teaching children all the answers' (and getting them through a certain type of examination) but such answers may be little more than verbalisms on the surface of the mind. True knowledge and understanding which become part of the pupils' interior mental life and convictions are arrived at by personal discovery. This kind of search and discovery, if it is to avoid mere subjectivism, calls for an approach which combines an openness to all kinds of evidence with methods of disciplined inquiry, all in an atmosphere of academic freedom.

At the same time, the anti-dogmatic approach which excludes the subjective aspect cannot be regarded as a satisfactory alternative, since this is more likely to lead to a misinterpretation of religious phenomena than to true understanding.

It has long been assumed, by believers and non-believers alike, that emotional involvement leading to commitment is inseparable from a truly informed and sympathetic study of religion. We believe this assumption to be false, and that an educational approach to this dimension of human experience can pay due regard to the subjective element in religion, in much the same way as musical appreciation includes some imaginative participation in the experience of the composer or the performer.

III. Recent writing and research in the field of religious education

There have been many far-reaching developments and changes in British society since 1944, and many of these have affected the general attitude to religion. This has been apparent, not only in the decline of support for the churches, and most other religious institutions, but in a changed attitude towards religion in schools.

'Secondary education for all' was followed by the introduction of 'the Welfare State', with improved health services and social security. Economic recovery from the War was accompanied by a wider distribution of affluence, the spread of the mass media of communication, advertising, and entertainment, teenage fashions, 'pop' culture, greater freedom and permissiveness in speech and conduct, increased opportunities for travel, and, since the Robbins Report,[31] a great expansion in opportunities for higher education. At the same time Britain's dominant role in world affairs had come to an end and there has been much uncertainty of purpose in national life. The influx of Asian, African, and West Indian immigrants has added to the complexity of this situation.

In addition to these social changes there have been changes of educational theory and practice, arising particularly from the findings of developmental psychology. These have already brought about dramatic changes in primary schools, and their importance is being increasingly recognized in secondary education. Every subject in the curriculum is being re-examined and re-structured. In religious education this reappraisal is particularly urgent; there is plenty of evidence that what ought to be a vital and exciting subject of study is often boring, stale, and ineffective.

Happily, these problems have been receiving a great deal of attention, particularly in the last decade.[32] This is not the place to attempt a summary of all that has been published in the last ten years, but it will be worth noting some of the main trends before going on to consider ways in which a new curriculum should be developed.[33] Three different conceptions of religious education may be discerned in the education reports, the new agreed syllabuses, and recent research monographs.

1. The 'neo-confessional' approach

The first conception of religious education in a multi-cultural society attempts to make 'confessional' or dogmatic religious education more acceptable and effective by improving methods and techniques in accordance with the findings of educational research, and especially by constructing syllabuses based on the capacities, needs and interests of the pupils. These attempts are usually liberal in intention, and at the secondary level their approach is often described as 'open-ended'. However, this is an 'open-ended' approach to Christianity. They generally acknowledge the need to introduce young people to other world religions and non-religious philosophies of life, but the place given to these in the syllabuses shows that they are regarded as tolerated extras to the officially approved viewpoint. Both the Plowden and the Newsom Reports,[34] and all the new agreed syllabuses,[35] adopt this position, and Dr R. J. Goldman has had enormous influence in establishing it in primary schools. Goldman applied Piaget's theories of mental development in children[36] to the development of their 'religious' thinking and found that much of the Biblical material taught to young children was unsuitable because it was unintelligible in terms of their experience, and presupposed capacities for thought and understanding not possessed by most children until a much later age.[37] Young children are not intellectually 'ready' for religious teaching in the adult sense until they have developed the capacity for abstract thought. According to Goldman, it is not until a child reaches the period of adolescence that he or she is 'intellectually ready to apprehend what is the Christian faith'.[38] The widespread rejection of religious belief at this age when, according to Goldman, it should have its maximum appeal, is due in large measure to the failure of religious educationists to take account of the processes of intellectual development and hence to teach too much too soon. Biblical and theological material has been presented to children when their intellectual equipment has been inadequate to comprehend it. The children have adapted the material to their conceptual capacities with the result that distortion, misunderstanding, and crude literalism have been instilled and religion has come to be associated in adolescence with these childish misconceptions. In addition, the continued diet of Bible study has become boring, and the impression that religion is irrelevant to real life has been confirmed by this constant reference to an ancient book and an ancient order of society.

According to Goldman the young child has no specifically 'religious' needs; he needs security and standards of behaviour, he has physical, intellectual, and emotional needs, but these cannot be held to be religious in the true sense of the word. He therefore proposes an across-subject approach to the education of young children in which RE lessons disappear and all work is the exploration of 'life themes'. The religious element is provided by relating the whole world of experience and discovery to the basic idea that this world is God's world.

> The Christian faith is a frame of reference through which everything can be experienced, related and interpreted.[39]

> I would lead children to integrate all they are learning and doing in all subjects within a world view of God as creator and as the person who cares about his people.[40]

Experientially-based and, where possible, spontaneous, worship is probably the most effective form of religious education at this age, according to Goldman. The Bible, instead of forming the basic content of religious education with young children should be used only very sparingly and then only to illustrate things arising from experiential work. More specific Bible teaching should only be introduced at the late junior stage although a study of life in Bible times can be started earlier.

Goldman condemns those who would use religion in education, as 'a pew fodder, citizenship fodder and democracy fodder device',[41] nevertheless, his presuppositions are still 'confessional':

> Christianity should be taught because it is true, because it answers the deepest needs of human nature, and without a knowledge of the love of God and a relationship with him men and women will live impoverished lives.[42]

This neo-confessionalism, though undoubtedly sincere, cannot be the basis of religious education in maintained schools; it is just as open to objection from non-Christian teachers as the old confessionalism.

The Plowden committee was divided in its report, a significant minority of its members arguing that traditional RE had no place in primary schools although teaching about the lives of great religious leaders and teachers of different faiths was desirable, and for cultural reasons Bible stories were perfectly appropriate.[43] However, the majority report endorsed the 'confessional' approach. After advising teachers to be 'honest and sincere' in their teaching and saying that a teacher 'should not pretend to beliefs he does not hold', it goes on to say

> children should be taught to know and love God and to practise in the school community the virtues appropriate to their age and environment.[44]

Non-Christian teachers with conscientious difficulties should, according to the Plowden Report, stress 'the ethics and history of Christianity rather than its

theology'.[45] Thus, despite a few concessions to liberalism like the recommenda-
tion that non-Christian sources might be used in assemblies and that minority
religious groups like the Muslims might be given separate facilities for worship,
the Plowden Report retains a thoroughly confessionalist position.

The Newsom Report makes many concessions to a more open approach. It is
strongly critical of purely academic Bible study and insistent that religious teaching should be made relevant to the needs of adolescents. It advocates an open
approach to the study and discussion of the ultimate questions of human
existence and affirms that 'the whole staff, irrespective of religious affiliations,
can make a united contribution to both the spiritual and moral development of
the pupils'.[46] Nevertheless, it is still confessionalist at heart, speaking of school
assemblies as times 'in which pupils and teachers seek help in prayer, express
awe and gratitude and joy, and pause to recollect the presence of God'.[47]

In various ways all the newer agreed syllabuses attempt to introduce greater
relevance and reality into religious education with a view to making it more
effective. This is immediately evident from the titles of at least four of them:
the new Lancashire syllabus (1968) is entitled *Religion and Life*; the Inner
London syllabus (1968), *Learning for Life*; Northampton's primary syllabus
(1968) is entitled *Fullness of Life* and sub-titled *An Exploration into Christian
Faith for Primary Schools*; the secondary syllabus is entitled *Life and Worship*.
They introduce many changes of approach along lines suggested by R. J.
Goldman and, for secondary schools, by Harold Loukes, yet all these syllabuses
remain Christian documents written by Christians and aiming at Christian
education. Moreover, their content is still predominantly biblical, although
some sections are much less so.

The West Riding syllabus (1966) is probably the most influential of the new
syllabuses and its approach is typical of the concern that religious education
should relate to the life and needs of the pupils. Instead of beginning with lofty
theological and religious objectives, it states the needs of children. These are
defined as:

> (a) a need for SECURITY, (b) a need for SIGNIFICANCE, (c) a need for
> STANDARDS, and (d) a need for COMMUNITY.[48]

These needs are met, says the syllabus, (*a*) when 'their physical and emotional
needs are satisfied and when they know they are cared for and understood';
(*b*) when 'as they learn that they are valued in their own right, they mature as
individuals with their own special gifts'; (*c*) when they are not merely aware of
rules but of a sense of values in the adults around them; and (*d*) when they learn
to live together through the experience of sharing and mutual relationships in
the school community.

32

The syllabus then adds:

> From the Christian point of view, these personal needs are religious needs which are only satisfied by the growing discovery that at the heart of the universe there is a God who cares, a spirit who seeks to enter into personal relationships with us. Ultimately it is this which gives us security and significance.

It goes on to point to Christ and the Church as the source and manifestation of Christian ethical standards and community values respectively. The syllabus sees the ideal school as a Christian community:

> Expressions of the Christian spirit should be found at many points in the life of the school in such qualities as kindness, constancy, truthfulness, patience, respect for others, good manners, loyalty, courtesy, industry, perseverance, reverence for beauty, truth and goodness and a tacit confidence in the grace of God.[49]

The Inner London syllabus (*Learning for Life*), which contains some of the most perceptive and sensitive comments on the problems of religious education in the contemporary world,[50] is none the less basically 'confessional' in its concern. It describes its objectives thus:

> This syllabus is not only concerned with Christianity as an abstract concept but with what it means in every sense to be a Christian and to be religiously committed.[51]

The same point could be made of any of the new syllabuses. They are not unaware of the problems involved in such an approach and are sometimes almost apologetic about it, but they are all Christian documents which assume that the fundamental objective of religious education is to inculcate Christianity. Most of them do their best to be liberal within these terms of reference: the Inner London syllabus, for example, recommends the study of the lives of 'men of all beliefs who have helped their fellow men'[52] for children in the 6 to 8 age range. Also, the lives of 'all who have contributed to the happiness and welfare of mankind, scientists, inventors, engineers, artists of all kinds, etc. . . .' and 'those who have fought for the rights and freedom of man'. The West Riding and the Lancashire syllabuses both include sections dealing briefly with other world religions at the late secondary stage. Even the Wiltshire syllabus (1967), the most explicitly confessional of all the new syllabuses, allows fourth- and fifth-formers to become acquainted with scientific Humanism and Marxism – but under the heading 'The world's challenge to the Church'. Then, lest any harm should have been done by these 'rival views of life's purpose', the remainder of the syllabus is devoted to a detailed examination of the Church's recent history, its contribution to social and humanitarian work, and its internal life and organization. This is then followed by a systematic study of Christian doctrine.[53]

2. The 'implicit religion' approach

The second conception of religious education in a multi-cultural society abandons the 'confessional' standpoint and concentrates on the development of what we have called 'implicit' religion. The advocates of this type of approach see religious education primarily as an unrestricted personal quest for meaning in life in terms of actual experience, assisted by dialogue between pupil and teacher. Such an approach consists less in the communication of information about religion than in an analysis of experience and the relating to it of appropriate material to broaden and deepen insight. Harold Loukes, the major exponent of this approach, has had great influence on religious education in secondary schools. Few writers on religious education have written with greater realism and common sense. His *Teenage Religion* and *New Ground in Christian Education*, published in 1961 and 1965, have helped to clear away a great deal of the wishful thinking that blinded teachers to what was happening in their own classrooms. The first book is the report of an inquiry which he carried out for the Institute of Christian Education. It is a frank and thorough examination of the religious attitudes, practices, and beliefs of pupils in secondary modern schools and their implications for religious education. The second book is a critique of the place of religion in schools based on further research findings, and a positive statement of Loukes' own position.

In both these books, Loukes' main interest is the non-academic majority of pupils in secondary schools, although the basic principles which underlie his thinking apply to all children. Loukes, who is Reader in Education at the University of Oxford, is a passionate advocate of 'learning through experience':

> Unless a subject proceeds from the concrete to the abstract, unless the whole process is set about with sense experience, returning perpetually to questions 'What are we talking about?' 'What do you see?', and 'What do you think about it?', then it will not be educative.[54]

Good teaching, for Loukes, is 'a process of dialogue about experience', and this must apply as much to religious education as to any other subject. In fact, it should apply even more to religious education than to any other form of education, since this subject is primarily concerned with the meaning and purpose of life in its totality. According to Loukes, religious education is at root 'a conversation between older and younger on the simple question, "What is life like?" '[55]

34

All subjects contribute something to the answer to this question, but while individual subjects reveal aspects of the fabric of life, religious education is concerned with the dimension of depth and meaning seen in and through all subjects.

> Science is concerned with the structure of crystals, religious education is concerned with wonder and delight, the response of the human spirit as microscopy throws up this beauty . . . Geography is concerned with the activities and structures of peoples and the way they came about by reason of situation and contour and climate and the way those came about; religious education is concerned with the human condition as it is experienced in such contours and climate, and thence to the Human Condition in its Climate and what account men can give of Situation and Contour.[56]

For Loukes, religious education is a unifying, all-embracing subject the content of which is:

> the depth, the realisation of everything, the experience of the whole, the living and the human, alongside the categorization and analysis, the selection and abstraction, that constitute academic disciplines.[57]

All subjects, according to Loukes, have their 'religious' dimension but a separate period should be set apart to consider and explore this dimension. He sees the Christian tradition as providing the framework in which this exploration should take place, but the Christian answers should not be imposed; the exploration should be spontaneous, arising from the children's experience and relating to it. Any study of the Bible

> . . . must start from the position that the Bible is not about the Bible but about the human situation and that in itself it claims no more authority than it carries to its hearers.[58]

The job of the teacher is to set children thinking and searching for meaning in an atmosphere of sympathetic dialogue. Whether or not the teacher is a Christian is of no importance so long as he is honest and sincere and is prepared to enter into genuine dialogue with his pupils. But his honesty has to be a genuine honesty:

> . . . not loyalty to the Agreed Syllabus or the official Christian statements, but honesty to what his own life has taught him even if at some points it runs counter to orthodoxy.[59]

Convinced Christians can claim no monopoly of the search for living truth,

35

nor of the longing to open children's eyes to the largeness of the human situation in its mystery, its dreams of progress and in the actual achievement at its best.[60]

A similar approach is advocated by Sir Richard Acland in his books, *We Teach them Wrong*[61] and *Curriculum or Life*.[62] Acland suggests that the term 'religion' is a handicap in schools and an inadequate name for this personal search for life's meaning and values. He suggests that the subject might be better termed the study of 'Life'.

This raises an interesting question about this whole approach. By concentrating on 'implicit' religion its advocates seem in practice both to include and to exclude much more than is generally meant by religious education. For Loukes, the word 'religious', when used adjectivally to qualify the noun 'education' is an umbrella word including within its scope aesthetics, ethics, philosophy, teleology, humanitarianism, and all aspects of human experience which involve any type of poetic, artistic, or mystical apprehension. At the same time he seems to give little place to specifically 'religious' studies in religious education.

> A lesson on spiders, an argument on Charles I, a study of the climate of Peru, the story of Oedipus: these are all as 'religious' as the story of Abraham if they are treated personally and set the hearers off into the depth; while the Nativity, the Passion, the martyrdom of Stephen are as irreligious as quadratic equations if they are treated on the surface.[63]

One agrees, in a way – but is too much being claimed? To describe as religion any 'quest for meaning' in life, poetic insight, artistic vision, etc., which involves no necessary reference to any transcendent spiritual order or being for its interpretive principle is surely doing violence to language. Many subjects of human concern can be interpreted religiously, but not all attempts at interpreting life can meaningfully or accurately be designated 'religious'.

3. The 'explicit religion' approach

The third conception of religious education in schools also abandons the 'confessional' position, but it takes as its field of study the 'explicit' phenomena of religion, Christian and non-Christian, rather than the 'implicit' meaning of secular experience. It also includes some study of alternatives to religious belief, like Marxism and Humanism. Ninian Smart, Edwin Cox, and J. W. D. Smith, in varying degrees and with varying emphases, advocate this type of approach.

Professor Ninian Smart, head of the Department of Religious Studies at

Lancaster, has pioneered a radically new approach to the study of religion at university level, with a considerable measure of success. He suggests that the principles underlying his work at university level are those needed in schools, and he has discussed these principles in *The Teacher and Christian Belief* and *Secular Education and the Logic of Religion*. As director of the current Schools Council Project on Religious Education in Secondary Schools his thinking has already contributed a great deal to this working paper, and important aspects of it will be considered later. The following paragraphs simply indicate his general approach and his view of the aims of religious education. In the final chapter of the second of the two works mentioned above, Smart refers to what he calls 'The present schizophrenia in religious education':

> The schizophrenia consists in the twin facts that Christian education is entrenched in our school system . . . and that the typical modern institution of higher education is secular – that is, it is neutralist in regard to religious and ideological commitment.[64]

In Smart's view the confessionalist approach to religious teaching in schools is neither justified by the pluralistic character of our society nor educationally viable since it breeds resentment in pupils:

> If children are hypersensitive about one thing, it is unfairness and if they are resistant about anything, it is boredom. The combination of boredom and unfairness in religious education in schools has helped to confirm a number of generations of sceptics and atheists . . .[65]

The study of religion should be governed by the same educational principles as any other subject. The aim of religious teaching in schools should not be to evangelize or to induct pupils into a predetermined religious viewpoint but to create 'certain capacities to understand and think about religion'.[66] He draws a useful distinction between teaching *that* and teaching *how*. Too much religious education has been in the form of authoritative teaching *that*:

> But the essence of education, I would suggest, is teaching *how*. Thus teaching history is vastly more than telling people when and how things happened. It should issue in the capacity to do history – to think historically, to judge about historical issues, to understand some of the forces at work in major historical events, etc. The person learns how to do something; he learns a skill. Is then religious education to be an exception . . . ?[67]

Smart notes that parents appear to want 'some sort of induction to Christianity and traditional morals for their children'.[68] However, such an induction need not offend against educational principles so long as it is 'open' and sym-

37

pathetic, and so long as other viewpoints, religious and non-religious, are accorded equally 'open' and sympathetic treatment.

Smart sums up his approach by suggesting five aims:

> First, religious education must transcend the informative.
>
> Second, it should do so not in the direction of evangelizing, but in the direction of initiation into understanding the meaning of, and into questions about the truth and worth of, religion.
>
> Third, religious studies do not exclude a committed approach, provided that it is open, and so does not artificially restrict understanding and choice.
>
> Fourth, religious studies should provide a service in helping people to understand history and other cultures than our own. It can thus play a vital role in breaking the limits of European cultural tribalism.
>
> Fifth, religious studies should emphasise the descriptive, historical side of religion, but need thereby to enter into dialogue with the parahistorical claims of religions and anti-religious outlooks.[69]

The ideal teacher of religion, in Smart's view, is one who is ready to portray sympathetically and without bias any viewpoint which he may be required to teach:

> The test of one who is teaching reasonably in a society such as ours is openness, not what his commitments are. The Humanist teacher should give some imaginative grasp of religion, just as the Christian teacher should be able to elicit from his pupils an appreciation of the forces of Humanism. The Christian should be able to teach Buddhist studies and to do so without judgemental attitudes. It should in any event be a cause of joy that there is good in others, not a defensive cause of sorrow and fear.[70]

Edwin Cox would agree with much of what Smart says but would probably weight any syllabus more heavily with specifically Christian teaching. He agrees that 'openness' in religious education will include a study of other world religions and of 'philosophies, such as Humanism and Marxism, which have maintained that adequate explanations (i.e. of existence) can be framed without reference to the supernatural'.[71]

The purpose of religious education, he says, is:

> . . . to help pupils to understand the nature of our present secular, pluralistic society, to help them to think rationally about the state and place of religion in it, to enable them to choose objectively and on sound criteria between the many conflicting religious statements that are made in a

pluralistic society, and to work out for themselves, and to be able cogently to defend, their own religious position or their rejection of the possibility of having one.[72]

In Cox's view, the proper aim of religious education is not simply to give children a sensitive and intelligent grasp of religion as a phenomenon in human life but:

> the giving to children of a religious view of life and then allowing them freely to make up their own minds how that view shall express itself both in belief and practice.[73]

When one asks what Cox means by 'a religious view of life', one finds that his approach differs from that of Smart. He conceives of it as a mixture of humanitarianism with the view that life has some 'overall purpose' which children should be encouraged to seek. From his writing on 'the inculcation of favourable attitudes' to religious teaching in primary schools it is clear that he has leanings towards the neo-confessional approach. In the light of Kenneth Hyde's research results,[74] he concedes that 'the demand that only sincerely religious people should teach the subject' is 'perhaps justified'.[75]

J. W. D. Smith's *Religious Education in a Secular Setting*[76] is particularly important not only for its shrewd and sensitive analysis of the present situation but also for its frankness and willingness to follow through the logical implications for religious education of contemporary thought in philosophy and theology as well as in psychology. Dr John Hull writes of this book:

> It is breaking almost entirely new ground in an attempt to establish British religious education on a neutral philosophical basis. We may even say that what Rudolph Bultmann did on the basis of Heidegger for New Testament theology, J. W. D. Smith has begun to do for religious education.[77]

Smith points out that most of the recent discussion about religious education has been between Christians, who have been debating the success of the last twenty-five years work, but that what is needed now is discussion between Christian educationists and their non-Christian colleagues about the educational (rather than the ecclesiastical) role of religion in schools.

The non-Christian, Smith says, does and will increasingly ask:

> Must learning for living be done within the pattern of Christian belief and life? Is a truly 'open' approach really compatible with Christian education?[78]

39

Elsewhere he says:

> It may be time for Christian educators to think and to speak primarily as educators.[79]

In chapter 7 he shows how the philosophy of religious education which was dominant in the nineteen-thirties and -forties emerged. Religion (i.e. Christianity) was to permeate all education, the whole school was to be a Christian community, education should foster the Christian way of life.

He then goes on to show that such a philosophy of religious education is no longer viable. 'Christian education' must give way to educationally motivated 'religious' teaching which should embody an objective study primarily of Christianity but also of other world religions adapted to the various capacities of age and ability groups. He also accepts the need for a 'life-centred' approach to religious and moral problems at all ages (citing Loukes), and sees religious education as dealing with basic concerns of human existence. The element of mystery in life, particularly that created by the awareness of death, cannot be ignored without some damage to the personality. Towards this mystery people respond either with fear or mistrust, or with confidence. The latter response is the most healthy, and the stress laid by child psychologists on the need for unselfish love if personal growth is to take place in a normal manner adds conviction to this conclusion:

> By encouraging the growth of trust and interpreting the meaning of love religious education can play a vital part in fostering growth towards the fullest maturity of which individual boys and girls may be capable.[80]

In primary schools Smith argues that religious education should abandon the 'confessionalist' approach and should aim to deepen the existential sense of wonder and mystery which, he adds, must be distinguished from the mystery of ignorance and superstition.[81] At the junior stage children should also be given some preliminary, factual, objective study of Christianity, for example, the life of Jesus, to facilitate later personal growth towards an understanding of love. One of his major concerns is to emphasize that religious concepts cannot be meaningful to children who have no experience of the human situations in which these concepts are actually used by religious people: 'When God is real to parents, the word God is meaningful to their children.'[82]

He offers some astute criticisms of the thematic material prepared under the editorship of R. J. Goldman. Understanding the *religious* significance of bread, for example – 'this is my body given for you' – depends on contact with self-giving people and with a desire to be good ('hungry for what is good') rather

40

than upon understanding how yeast works and how bread is made and transported, today and in Palestine.

The content of secondary-school religious and moral education will be partly discussion of pupils' life problems. This, Smith suggests, should be conducted by a team of counsellors and religious specialists from various religious and non-religious backgrounds. The personal beliefs of teachers will not be very important:

> Their personal convictions might be strong but their professional concern for tolerance and freedom of opinion should be stronger.[83]

A factual study of Christianity is important, though this should not become 'an open-ended approach to a closed system of belief and practice'.[84] Insights from other religions are important, too. At the same time, on the final page, J. W. D. Smith says that, although bringing pupils to an awareness of the mystery of existence will *begin* to fulfil the aims appropriate to religious education today, 'the Christian interpretation of the mystery at the frontiers of human existence'[85] is that which will *fulfil* these aims. A concealed apology for Christianity runs through the book, despite the author's wish to avoid this. Christianity, because of its unique emphasis on love in human life, is particularly well suited to assist in the elucidation of the mystery of life and to contribute to personal growth:

> Such talking (between Christians and non-Christians about the place of religious education in state schools) can only be done meaningfully on the basis of our common human predicament and a recognition of elements in our common Christian inheritance which may still be acknowledged by all.
>
> All human knowledge and experience leads ultimately to the frontiers of mystery impenetrable by the human intellect. Awareness of that mystery and adaptation to it are necessary elements in man's growth to maturity. In this sense, at least, religion must have an enduring place in the educational curriculum.
>
> An important further step seems possible. The word love is central to our Christian inheritance and its contemporary relevance is universally acknowledged. Deeper insight into the 'riddle of a life lived and a death died' might help to clarify the true nature of agape and to expose the distinctive Christian insight into human nature and human relationships and, indeed, into our human situation.
>
> Here too Christians and non-Christians might find common ground on which to explore an 'open' approach to our Christian heritage.[86]

J. W. D. Smith combines the position of Harold Loukes with that of Ninian Smart. For the former religious education is a personal search for meaning conducted in an atmosphere of open dialogue. For the latter it is primarily an academic discipline, a dialogue with religion and religions. Smith's view is that the future of the subject must include both of these emphases.

IV. Aims and objectives

The foregoing discussion of three interpretations of the term 'religious education' also indicates three general aims, the 'confessional', the 'personal quest', and the objective or 'phenomenological'.

We take the view that the 'confessionalist' aim, though perfectly proper within a community of faith, is not appropriate within schools serving a multi-belief society.[87] Moreover, it conflicts at several points with the principles on which education is based.

> A great change in the concept of religious education has taken place during the last quarter of a century. The modern RE teacher is concerned to teach children to think, to question, and to discuss, as against encouraging them to receive ideas and information passively – the educational mode of former times.

> The modern teacher is also concerned to extend the child's awareness to include many forms of man's religious strivings instead of concentrating on Christianity alone. Another important change is that moral education is no longer regarded as synonymous with RE.[88]

We incline to the view that religious education must include both the personal search for meaning and the objective study of the phenomena of religion. It should be both a dialogue with experience and a dialogue with living religions, so that the one can interpret and reinforce the other. Within this wider context 'confessional' teaching should sometimes be heard, both as part of the evidence in the study of a given religion (for example, Protestant Christianity) and as part of the dialogue between the pupils and the world in which they live.

> It is not right that controversial religious material should be kept outside school. Teaching must be meaningful and existential, not dull and harmless, and this means bringing in even what is controversial. But religious material is difficult to handle and needs special training of the teachers. A teacher of history dealing mainly with political and economic history is not the right man to deal with the history of religions. A teacher of literature, skilled in novels and lyrics, may not be the right man to teach about the basic religious texts. And moral abstracts from religion do not give a true description of what religion is. Teaching of religion has to be a separate subject, because the teachers need special training.[89]

Such training should equip them, not only to handle religious matters sensitively and with perception, but also to handle the classroom situation in such a way that, although 'confessionalist' views are given a proper hearing they are not allowed to override or inhibit the pupils' free spirit of inquiry.

> . . . the recognition of alternative possibilities of belief and practice is essential. This is not to affirm that all such possibilities are true, or valid, or equally desirable. It is not inconsistent even with some existing historic religion being the one true and ultimate faith. If there is such a faith, it should be able to win its way among the other possibilities in a fair show of evidence. The devoted study of alternative orientations, from a variety of disciplined perspectives, should only serve to vindicate the true faith in competition with its false rivals.[90]

In any attempt to frame an adequate curriculum it is logically and educationally wrong to begin the process by considering the lesson content. Before it is possible to decide on content and method the general aims of the exercise must be analysed and sub-divided into a series of specific objectives. On pages 16 to 19 of this working paper we listed the general aims of religious education as conceived by a number of important commissions and committees concerned with this aspect of education. Although these statements represent many religious viewpoints and a variety of academic interests there is a remarkable harmony between them. This consensus as to the aims of religious education is impressive. We would not presume to summarize, but it is helpful in the present discussion to list some of the main strands: religious education seeks to promote awareness of religious issues, and of the contribution of religion to human culture in general; it seeks to promote understanding of religious beliefs and practices, it also aims to awaken recognition of the challenge and practical consequences of religious belief. Like all liberal education it is concerned that such awareness and understanding should be founded on accurate information, rationally understood and considered in the light of all relevant facts.

These general aims can be broken down further and more particularly as follows (and here we also give *examples* – instances of the kind of objectives the teacher may have when devising a course of study).

1   *Awareness of religious issues*
    (a) *explicit* issues – e.g. the capacity to understand the reasons for differences of religious belief, for instance within the Christian tradition.
    (b) *implicit* issues – e.g. the capacity to explore music with a view to seeing whether it can give one new insights into the nature of the world; and, if so, the connexion of these with questions about the 'purpose' of life.

2 *Awareness of the contribution of religion to human culture*
   e.g. acquiring knowledge of the ways in which the Christian heritage has influenced social life in different parts of the UK.

3 *Capacity to understand beliefs*
   e.g. understanding the Muslim conception of Allah, and the type of language employed to express this.

4 *Capacity to understand practices*
   e.g. understanding what worshipping is intended to do, and the use of symbolism in it.

5 *Awareness of the challenge of religious belief*
   e.g. the capacity to form a well-informed judgement about Christian or atheistic belief.

6 *Awareness of the practical consequences of religious belief*
   e.g. capacity to understand issues raised by pacifist elements in, for instance, the Christian and Buddhist traditions.

Educational objectives have been defined as 'changes in pupil behaviour which it is intended to bring about by learning'. Although they are concerned with the development of certain cognitive skills, attitudes, and interests, it is evident from the examples given that this involves the acquisition of accurate, factual information.

These general objectives need to be broken down even further before a particular teaching unit can be devised. Such 'specific educational objectives' will vary from one teaching situation to another – and they must be worked out by the teachers concerned; but they must be arrived at by considering three main factors:

Information about the level of development of the pupils, their needs and interests, must be taken into account. The social conditions and problems which the children are likely to encounter provide a second source of data. And thirdly, there is the nature of the subject-matter and the types of learning that can arise from study of the subject-matter.[91]

The important thing to realize is that specific objectives provide the real starting-points for syllabus planning. They begin to suggest methods and contents – the kind of behaviour and the activities in which the pupil must engage if the required development is to take place. They also provide the real basis for any attempts to assess the teaching's effectiveness.

V. Content and methods

Not only objectives, but the teaching material that flows from them, must be derived from careful consideration of:

a the psychological capacity of the pupils, their interests and needs;
b the social conditions and problems which the pupils are likely to encounter;
c the nature of the subject-matter and the types of learning that can arise from it.

Much has been, and is being, written on the first and second of these considerations.[92] For example, results have just been published of careful research carried out in Sweden to ascertain the real interests of 15-year-old pupils. This was an attempt to see how the revised syllabuses of religious teaching in the upper levels of the compulsory school could be made relevant to the real-life problems of the pupils. The conclusion was that:

> questions which might be termed existential were regarded as important, while questions expressed in traditional Christian terminology were regarded as unimportant. Important were questions about life and death (how life is created, the moral right to take life, life after death), about race and social equality, about war and peace, about suffering and evil, about solitude and companionship, about sex and family, about faith and reason. Unimportant were questions about Jesus and salvation, about church and confession, about prayer and sacrament.[93]

This research was carried out with one age group in one country. Similar results have been reached with the same age group in Britain[94] and with older pupils.[95] It would appear that, though the existential questions are verbalized in different ways at different ages and in different cultures, they are not dependent on age or cultural environment. They are timeless questions and, in the Western world at least, of universal concern.

The third of the three considerations listed at the beginning of this section has not received so much attention. However, for purposes of curriculum development, this can be even more helpful. It is discussed at length in *Secular Education and the Logic of Religion*.[96]

Smart points out that it is necessary first to distinguish between the 'historical' approach to religious data and the 'parahistorical'. The 'historical' approach is purely descriptive and is concerned with what is publicly demonstrable. The 'parahistorical' approach sees events as relevant to, or enshrining insights about, the nature of reality. Smart illustrates the distinction by reference to the joke about the man who asked another 'Do you believe in baptism?' 'Believe in it?' the other man replied, 'I've seen it done'.

> The question of whether Jesus lived in Galilee is, on this usage, an historical question; but the question of whether he died for men's sins is parahistorical (but note that the question of whether he thought he died for men's sins reverts to the historical side). The question of whether mystical experience contains an unvarying central core is an historical question; but the question of whether one knows God through mystical experience is a parahistorical one. The problem of the degree to which a particular religion is sociologically determined is an historical problem (on this usage); the question of whether its moral teachings are right is a parahistorical question.[97]

Traditionally, in Western education, a religion has been treated chiefly as a system of beliefs with an associated code of conduct. This is perhaps the chief reason why the study of 'comparative religions' has almost always been relegated to the final years of secondary schooling, when powers of abstract thinking have developed. But such an approach to religion is terribly inadequate. Religions have many aspects, some of which may be studied at quite an early age, and all of which must be studied if true understanding free from distortion is the aim of education. For example, when studying a given religion, one might distinguish first the 'observable' aspects – ritual, custom, buildings, books, etc. One might then study the teaching of the religion, the ideas and beliefs which underlie the observable aspects. After this one could go on to discover what these external phenomena mean to the people involved in and committed to the religion – the 'experiential' or existential aspect. In fact, without this data, a true understanding and appreciation of the religion would be impossible.

Smart emphasizes that religion is multi-dimensional. It has, in fact, six major dimensions:[98]

1 *Doctrinal:* Most religions have official teaching or doctrines. Christianity, for example, teaches the doctrine of the Trinity; Hinduism the doctrines of karma and transmigration, and Buddhism the Four Noble Truths.

2 *Mythological:* Religions usually express their beliefs in story form, sometimes stories based upon actual historical events, sometimes fictional stories with symbolic religious meaning. Whether they be stories of God, of the gods, or of a venerated religious leader or teacher, such stories generally express convictions about the religious significance of life or the

47

activity of the divine in human affairs. These stories may be termed 'myth'.[99] The story of the Fall in the Book of Genesis, the Hindu epic, the Ramayana, and the Birth Tales of the Buddha are narratives of this sort.

3 *Ethical:* Religions prescribe principles, and sometimes codes, of moral conduct. These are usually related to the doctrinal and mythological teaching. The first epistle of John justifies its ethical demands by reference to the Christian interpretation of the life and death of Jesus; Mahayana Buddhism calls for a life directed to 'the pure love of creatures' as an expression of gratitude for the condescension and concern shown by the Buddhas in the mythological 'Lotus of the Good Law'.

These three dimensions together represent the general standpoint and world view of a religion, but they are not likely to come to life and be properly understood unless they are seen in their context – and that context is the living practice of the faith. This in turn has three dimensions:

4 *Ritual:* In this dimension Smart includes all specifically religious actions; not only such acts as celebrating the Christian sacraments but also closing one's eyes in prayers, turning towards Mecca, touching a 'mezuzah' on the doorpost, treading the Eightfold Path, etc. All of these actions, in different ways, are responses to the transcendental or the divine.

5 *Experiential:* Religious faith is founded upon, and sustained by, intuitive insight. It may be a dramatic experience like the Enlightenment of the Buddha, the vision of Isaiah in the Temple, or the conversion of St Paul. At a humbler level countless religious men and women would speak of moments of illumination, insight, conversion, a sense of presence and so on. Sometimes these were catalytic experiences, bringing about great changes of outlook and behaviour; sometimes they served simply to confirm existing faith. This, perhaps more than any other, is the element that makes a religion a living faith.

6 *Social:* Although the continuance and development of religion may be nurtured by inward experience, it is also sustained by the company of fellow-believers, like the Church in Christianity and the Sangha in Buddhism.

These six 'dimensions of religion' are interrelated and interdependent. So long as this is borne in mind, and the interrelations traced, they suggest six different starting-points for the study of a given religion. How this may be done is currently being explored by a number of serving teachers who are assisting the present project (see Chapter X).

Obviously, if pupils are to be aware of the social dimension of Islam, or the ritual dimension of Hinduism, talk alone will not suffice (although a gifted believer in one of these faiths may be able to communicate much by drawing on the experiential dimension). What is needed is a stay in a Muslim country, or in India, with opportunities to observe, listen, ask questions, share the sense of community, the excitement, the solemnity, and so on. Unfortunately, such opportunities of direct experience are not likely to come the way of most pupils. Ways must, therefore, be found, by the use of second-hand and third-hand experience, to recreate as much of that primary encounter as possible. For example, a good film of the Hajj, the great Pilgrimage, can convey something of the Muslim sense of brotherhood. This could be reinforced, and modified, by other resource materials – key verses from the Qur'an or other Muslim poetry, a novel written from the Muslim point of view, a visit from someone who has made the Hajj, current news and photographs from Arab countries, information illustrative of the great contribution of Islam to the history and culture of mankind, etc.

If some teachers view this as a very difficult kind of teaching to prepare, it should be pointed out that it is a much less complex operation than trying to get children to appreciate the religious situation in Israel in the eighth century BC, or even the religious import of the journeys of St Paul.

It should also be a matter of serious concern that, since the majority of pupils in secondary schools do not share in the life and worship of a Christian church, they are not likely to gain a true understanding of the Christian religion, unless well-designed 'substitute' learning-experiences form part of the teaching.

Religion cannot be understood simply from the outside. It is like stained-glass windows in the cathedrals. You see them from the outside, and they are nothing, grey and colourless. You see them from the inside, and they are wonderful, full of life and colour. Unless they are understood as seen from the inside religious dogmas and rituals seem grey and sapless, if not absurd. Teachers need, therefore, to observe, in all references to religious beliefs and religious activities what Smart calls 'the principle of intentionality':

> Certain of the descriptive terms we use, conditioned by our own cultural and religious heritage, are laden with judgments. Every time some external value judgment of this kind occurs, it involves a betrayal of what I shall call the 'principle of intentionality'. Let me explain this briefly as follows: In describing a human activity, we only describe fully and correctly if we include in the description the meaning the activity has for the person or persons participating. It is strictly a misdescription if I say that a person is praying to a statue, if he conceives himself as praying to Vishnu. Thus

D

description must include reference to the intentions and beliefs, etc., of those who engage in them. This is what I mean by the principle of intentionality.

The task then of description in religion is in part to bring out the meanings and values present to the participants. This task is obscured and frustrated when external meanings and values are imposed upon them. Thus, in an important sense, the study of a religion involves *presenting* that faith, and so the exercise frequently involves considerable powers of sensitivity and imagination.[100]

Before leaving the subject of content and method, it is important to examine the relationships between educational objectives and specific teaching units. We incline to the view that, although some units of work flow naturally from a given educational objective, too mechanical a development of teaching units from one or two specific objectives is to be avoided. We think it better to select units of work that flow naturally from the three considerations listed at the head of this section, especially the needs, interests, and abilities of the pupils, and then to note the educational objectives they are likely to serve. Preference should then be given to those units which are most likely to develop progress in understanding and in the relevant skills. Worth-while units of work generally have several objectives in view, and their effect is cumulative, so that progress towards these objectives develops over a series of units spread over a considerable time. This can be illustrated by considering the six objectives listed above (pp.44–5) and then examining some typical teaching units to see which, if any, of these objectives they are likely to serve.

Examples of teaching units
1   *Creation and evolution:* the myths of creation from various sources including Genesis 1 and 2. Current scientific accounts of the origin of the universe and of life upon the Earth.
     i.e. wrestling with questions of cosmology, considering the differing contribution of scientific and religious thinking, identifying one kind of religious language (i.e. myth), beginning to discover the nature of one kind of biblical literature.

2   *Some of the poetry of religion:* for example, two or three psalms, the words of hymns, 'Gitanjali', some religious poetry from non-Christian sources. The use of poetry in devotion and liturgy, attempts to write modern psalms.
     i.e. discovering another form of religious language and other parts of the Bible. Considering the existential and the devotional aspects of religion, developing one's own poetic response to religious ideas and experiences.

50

3   *The mystery of suffering:* the response of various religious and non-religious
    thinkers to the presence of pain and suffering in the world. For example,
    Job, Gautama – the Buddha, the New Testament Kerygma, Camus and
    Sartre.
    i.e. exploring their own and other men's experience and noting its implica-
    tions for religious doctrine.

4   *The religious community:* 'The idea of the People of God' in the Old
    Testament and in the New Testament, the Buddhist Sangha, Monastic
    Orders, exclusivism and universalism, the protest of the authors of Jonah,
    Job, and Ruth, serving communities, teaching communities.
    i.e. growing in understanding of the community dimensions of religion.
    The relation of religious communities to society as a whole. Exploring
    other forms of religious language – story and drama, and discovering fresh
    parts of the Bible.

5   *Enlightenment:* how inspiration or guidance is said to come. For example,
    angels in Luke, dreams in Matthew, a voice from Heaven at the baptism
    and temptation of Jesus and the conversion of Paul, a voice from the burn-
    ing bush to Moses, a voice in the Temple to Isaiah, the Quaker 'inner
    light', advice of experts or friends, common sense, etc. Enlightenment in
    Hinduism, Buddhism, Taoism, etc.
    i.e. investigation of the experiential dimension of religion, discovering a
    further form of language used by religion – symbolism, sampling the
    doctrinal element of Eastern religions, etc.

6   *Personal relationships – popularity and alienation:* differences between people,
    individual talents, 'all children are special', reasons for popularity, physical,
    psychological, etc., groups, gangs, teams, friends, the social isolate, the
    second Christian commandment, 'loving enemies', racial, cultural and
    sub-cultural groupings, and tensions.
    i.e. growth in awareness of factors that unite or divide society, considera-
    tion of the ethical dimension of Christianity (could be extended to include
    ethical standards of other religious and non-religious groups, for example,
    Humanism).

It will be observed that these educational objectives and teaching units are
more concerned to deepen understanding and to develop cognitive skills than to
inform about separate facts. There is a place for the accumulation of facts, but
this is incidental to the learning process and not a substitute for it. They are,
perhaps, best gathered up at the end, when their nature is understood, rather
than introduced in verbal form at too early a stage. For example, it is possible,

51

even in a junior school, to teach children the 'facts' about the varied types of literature in 'the Bible library'. Most of this information, however, will be merely a string of verbalisms until they have developed the mental capacity, and have had the opportunity to explore, the various types of literature, for example by sharing in units of work like the first three listed above.

VI. Related fields of study: integrated studies

What we have termed 'implicit' religion may feature in discussion at almost any point in the school day, and teachers of many disciplines will be contributing, one way or another, to their pupils' searches for answers to religious questions. For example, a good biology teacher will be willing to discuss with the pupils their qualms about vivisection, even though this is not really part of the academic study of biology.

However, 'explicit' manifestations of religion are not likely to feature in the normal teaching of some school subjects. This is true of mathematics, natural sciences, and language study, as well as the various skills such as reading, writing, and physical education. There are, however, several other disciplines that are directly concerned with religious matters and that cannot be taught responsibly without taking account of religion as part of human existence.[101]

The richest opportunities occur in the study of literature. One of the chief aims of literary study is to acquaint pupils with examples of writings that have played an important role in human civilization. Among these are the literature of the great religions of mankind, particularly their sacred scriptures. In Britain considerable emphasis should be placed on the Bible as one of the major resources of Western civilization. Pupils should also have some acquaintance with the sacred literature of other religions like the Talmud, the Qur'an, and the Bhagavadgita. Obviously the treatment of the Bible will include such matters as analysis of language structure and style, the probable dates of composition and authorship, and the historical and cultural context out of which the various writings came. These critical methods, however, are merely tools that may enable the pupil to understand better what the writings mean. Religious writings are verbal expressions of faith, and sacred books are collections of writings that have proved unusually powerful in expressing the faith of a historic religious community. Therefore one can understand religious literature only by an actual or imaginative participation in the community of faith from which the literature came. The central meanings of the Bible may be comprehended only in the light of the faith of the people for whom the writings were a sacred disclosure. Its significance cannot be measured in terms of its message to persons for whom it is not the Bible (i.e. a testament of faith).

A teacher's own interpretation of what the Bible says does not constitute an objective study of it, nor is a teacher objective in interpreting it according to some viewpoint that happens to be current in the literary world. Sacred writings have to be interpreted in the light of their significance to the community of faith to which they were addressed. For example, the story of Daniel in the Bible is not simply the story of one man's personal courage. It has to be understood in the light of Israel's abiding faith in the power of God to over-rule all human opposition and to fulfil the divine purposes for his people. Although the particular occasion for this affirmation of trust was Antiochus Epiphanes' desecrations in Judea about 168 BC, the story's setting is the time of the Exile in Babylon (586 BC–) and its message has remained a source of encouragement through the ages to a people faced time and again with threats to their security and integrity as a community of faith. Similarly, the ethical teachings of Jesus cannot adequately be interpreted from the literary point of view as a collection of moral exhortations. As literature, they belong to the Gospels. The ethical teachings of Jesus are integral to the faith of the primitive Christian community, and to the religious conviction that in the person of Jesus, God had decisively intervened in human affairs to bring light and life to a world struggling in darkness and against the fear of death. Any competent teacher of literature knows how to interpret writings in terms of the uses for which they are intended. Religious literature is no exception.

Next to literature, music and art are most likely to include some study of religion. Every religious tradition has expressed its faith in aesthetic objects. Sacred music, religious painting and sculpture, church architecture, sacred dances are all outward expressions of religious feelings and religious beliefs. To understand these creations it is not sufficient merely to study their technical design – form, material, medium, style, etc. It is also necessary to project oneself imaginatively into the world of thought and feeling inspired by faith. A Gothic cathedral cannot be understood apart from the particular faith of the community that built it; a Negro spiritual cannot be truly appreciated apart from the profound religious experience of the oppressed racial group that gave it birth. In music education it is right that children of all faiths and no faith should be introduced to great hymns, anthems, cantatas, and other forms of church music, as a means of understanding the religious aspirations of the community that produced them, not as a means of persuading pupils to adopt that religious outlook. The same applies to the study of the music, dance–drama, and art of other religions. Objectivity is not achieved by searching for some presumably neutral outlook; the key to understanding is to enter imaginatively into the faith of the believers.

A third subject which includes the study of religion is history. Because religion has been a major force in human events, no responsible teacher of history can ignore it. Religious institutions, events, and personalities have played, and still play, a prominent part in the affairs of mankind. It is not the function of the history teacher to inculcate a particular view of the meaning of human events, i.e. to teach his pupils 'the lessons of history'. As a historian his aim is to give, as far as possible, a balanced account of what happened, and as a teacher to train his pupils in the same objectivity. In this he will help them to use the evidence from the past to gain a sympathetic understanding of how people in other times and circumstances have thought, felt, and acted.

Since the evidence is never sufficient to give a full and conclusive account of events, historians have to be content with hypotheses. For example, there are many theories as to the causes of the Protestant Reformation. It does not follow, however, that a good Roman Catholic, or a Protestant, historian will necessarily prefer a theory which accords with his own ecclesiastical commitment. History is not partisan; it is a scholarly exercise with its own standards of objective inquiry. In seeking to ascertain the truth about any religious event one important qualification is the ability to enter sympathetically into the thoughts and feelings of religious believers.

Before considering ways of combining religious education with subjects like literature, art, music, history (and other subjects like geography and the behavioural and social sciences) two points should be emphasized:

1   Although the subjects are all studies of human affairs, and are all concerned with the pursuit of objective understanding, they are nevertheless distinct from one another; each has its own type of knowledge, its own logical structure, its own methods of inquiry and its own principles of verification.

2   These subjects also draw upon insights provided by the others. Narrow specialist teaching formerly associated with some university courses is unsuitable for use in schools, not only because it is an exercise too abstract for any but the brightest pupils, but also because it cannot hope to arrive at true understanding. For that the dimensions offered by related disciplines must be added.

In recent years there has been a cautious movement in secondary schools away from the old 'fragmented' type of curriculum towards a 'holistic' approach. This movement was given considerable support by the central position given to it by some writers in a number of working papers and reports from Schools Council projects and from Subject Committees.[102] The proposal to raise the school-leaving age provided a stimulus for a reappraisal of the secondary-school curriculum. In particular, attention has been directed to the problem of counteracting the apathy of pupils who will not take any public examination but will be required to spend an additional year in school. By concentrating on the interests and needs of these 'early leavers' it became apparent that subject divisions in the time-table were an artificial restriction. They either divided learning into a series of unrelated and not very relevant units, or made for a great deal of duplication of subject-matter. It was decided to select themes relevant to the pupils and to investigate them from the points of view of a number of subjects grouped under the general heading of the 'humanities' – geography, history, literature, the arts, and religious education. Sometimes attempts were made to link some of these with some of the natural sciences or the social sciences, and many different types of 'combined studies', 'integrated studies', 'social studies', 'general studies' and 'related studies' are to be found in secondary schools today.

This concern to restore a sense of unity to learning is not new. Over three hundred years ago Comenius was declaring his conviction that 'all truth is one – and leads to God':

> Metaphysicians sing to themselves alone, natural philosophers chant their own praise, astronomers dance by themselves, ethical thinkers make their laws for themselves, politicians lay their own foundations, mathematicians rejoice over their own triumphs, and theologicans rule for their own benefit. Yea, men introduce even into the same field of knowledge and science contradictory principles whereby they build and defend whatever pleases them, without much troubling themselves about the conclusions derived from the premises of other men.[103]

In our own time, however, the danger of over-specialization is far greater. The application of scientific methods of inquiry in all fields has led to a 'knowledge explosion', with increasing fragmentation. It is not only possible for study to get hopelessly out of touch with everyday life, but the development of the student can be terribly one-sided and inadequate. As C. P. Snow put it:

> It is rather as though, over an immense range of intellectual experience, a whole group was tone deaf. Except that this tone deafness doesn't come by nature but by training, or rather absence of training.[104]

In *Crisis in the Humanities* it was recognized that the ethos of the present age differs substantively from that prior to the two world wars. This is predominantly a scientific–technological age:

> Basically we must appreciate that the nineteenth-century classifications of knowledge are not always appropriate to our day, and we must see the danger of projecting those dimensions of learning – necessary at a high level

of scholarship and research – down to the lower levels in the schools, where they often become artificial, obsolete and harmful . . .

We must realise the limitations of an educational system in which we tend to abstract out of life instead of contracting in.[105]

A. N. Whitehead, writing on the same subject, concludes:

The solution which I am urging, is to eradicate the fatal disconnection of subjects which kills the vitality of our modern curriculum. There is only one subject matter for education, and that is life in all its manifestations. You may not divide the seamless coat of learning.[106]

In religious education this is very much the approach of Harold Loukes and Richard Acland:

Our main failure lies in the fact that we do not offer adolescents in our schools any introduction to what is going on in the world where they will have to work and live; nor any understanding of what is happening at present to the human race of which they are members.

Regrettably the school curriculum has been . . .

An almost random collection of separate bits and pieces leading to no coherent view of life as a whole.[107]

On the other hand, Paul Hirst, in Working Paper 12, emphasizing that learning must be clearly related to the logical structure of the relevant field of knowledge, seems to prefer teaching by subjects.[108] This is paralleled, in the field of religious education, by the approach of Ninian Smart, Edwin Cox and J. W. D. Smith.

Here, as elsewhere, we incline to the view that both approaches are needed. We would relate this, however, to Smart's distinction between teaching *that* and teaching *how*. Education does not begin with the assumption that there is a fixed and recognized corpus of knowledge which is immediately applicable to every generation. Rather it assumes that each generation must examine the data anew to determine what is important and what meets contemporary needs. This examination for relevance must be a continuous and on-going process, drawing both on the past and on the present. Education is a process that gives children the mental skills for this task; it is not just a process for supplying facts:

Schools Council Working Paper 11 emphasized this:

. . . the early school leaver is at best apathetic, at worst resentful and rebellious at the history, geography and religious education which appear on his time-table and yet seem to him to have nothing to do with the adult world he is soon to join.

A frequent excuse of failure seems to be that the course is often based on the traditional belief that there is a body of content for each separate subject which every young school leaver should know.[109]

We have tried to show that it is not the corpus of knowledge ('the body of content') that is distinctive of an academic discipline, but the form of thought, the way of interpreting experience, and the dialogue that logically flows from this. It would be generally agreed, for example, that the discourse we call 'religious' is not like that involved in scientific explanation; adoption of a religion is not the same as adopting a moral code; and religious beliefs are not the same as beliefs in ordinary historical facts. If these distinctions are clearly recognized then the 'thematic' approach may be used to develop mental skills in a number of subject disciplines without making artificial divisions in the subject-matter.

The school anticipating the adoption of integrated studies, whether on a large or small scale, does well to plan ahead. Many large educational questions have to be faced, and many basic organizational problems – the allocation of rooms for the course, the 'blocking' of sufficient time on the time-table, the provision of adequate resource material. All this suggests that plans should start at least a year in advance. Four practical points need watching from the standpoint of religious education:

1 The emphasis placed upon RE: time-table arrangements for the course may be very different from the regular pattern in the past, particularly if blocks of time are allocated to it. There should, however, be a comparable weighting of contribution by the subject over the academic year as a whole.

2 The effective presence of religious education in integrated studies:

> The course will operate in the periods formerly allotted to history, geography, English literature, and religious education. It will be organised and staffed by members of the history, geography, and English departments.[110]

No comment!

3 The role of the RE teacher in integrated studies: even though many such studies have little 'explicit' religious content the RE specialist is needed. This work may require even greater understanding and expertise than in the traditional lesson. If a teacher of another subject is expected to carry out an integrated scheme of study with a class entirely on his own, he should have access to a

58

resource bank of relevant material and to a colleague who can give specialist advice.

4 Personal relationships: integrated studies call for staff teamwork and rapport far more than the fragmented curriculum. It means entering 'each other's academic territory' and entering 'each other's minds and hopes and beliefs about what general humanity is'.[111] Success or failure will largely depend on team cooperation. Similarly, much depends on the relationship between the teachers and the pupils.

These practical considerations are important, but there are others which are more fundamental. These concern the actual conception and planning of the course.

1 The teacher who plans an integrated course of study must be coherent and articulate about the distinctive characteristics of his own discipline or subject in order to enlist the cooperation and sympathy of specialists in other fields. The current uncertainty as to the nature of RE, RK, RI, scripture, divinity, theology, etc., make this particularly difficult. That is one reason why religious education is often assigned no clear role in integrated studies – or is simply brought in when God, Jesus, the Church, the Bible, missionaries, or hymns are involved – which is not often!

2 Teachers of the different disciplines must examine carefully where the subjects converge – the logical connexions and relationships between the different areas of knowledge, a task far more complex than that of discovering common subject-matter.

3 Each teacher must see that the quality of the work contributed in his field is of a proper standard. There is a danger that integrated schemes can result in a watering down of all that is distinctive in a particular subject. Areas of study should not be chosen in a haphazard fashion, simply in view of the pupils' interest for example, but should be chosen carefully in accordance with educational objectives and to meet the structural requirements of the subjects involved.

4 Educational aims and objectives should be clear from the outset. In an integrated course common objectives have to be found, perhaps arising from those points where the subjects converge, as well as some that belong more specifically to the individual fields of study.

5 In crossing subject boundaries and following a common theme there should be no artificial juxtaposition of ideas or contrived situations to bring in materials that do not really belong but are deemed necessary knowledge. Integration must be inevitable, not clever.

6 No one subject can lay claim to be the unifying factor in an integrated study. The point of such a study is that, although the subject-matter is common to all, there are a number of distinctive ways of seeing it, each with its own characteristic way of understanding human experience and each having its own logical structure. Thus no subject can claim to include all the others. Theology was once known as 'the queen of the sciences'. No such claim can be made today. RE needs to be particularly aware of this temptation: the current trend that equates religion with life, and the appearance of 'life-themes' within the context of the RE lesson may, especially at primary-school level, sound like a 'take-over bid' for the entire curriculum – a reassertion that theology is, after all, the queen of the sciences and that things have not altered substantially since Aquinas.

Teachers who are considering the introduction of integrated studies might begin by considering the following questions:

a In general terms what are our aims in religious education? Can they be achieved through integrated studies?

b Can the various dimensions of religion receive adequate attention in integrated studies or do they constitute a type of material which is best taught separately?

c How adequately have published integrated schemes, to date, dealt with the religious dimension?

d What is the place of the RE specialist in integrated teaching?

e If religious issues are to receive adequate treatment in an integrated course, do we need to be able to assume that the pupil has a good grounding in religious education prior to the course, or is it enough for interest to arise via the integrated scheme and the pupil then to be directed to appropriate sources of information?

Integrated studies are still in the early, experimental stage. At their best they can absorb the interest and energies of 'early leavers' in a way that was rarely possible in the 'fragmented' curriculum. However, they are complex and there is still much to be learned about them, particularly where they involve religious education. As a previous publication put it:

> [the] most pressing need was to evolve ways of handling the 'areas of experience' which enabled the religious dimension to emerge clearly and naturally as an integral element of life, and thus carry their pupils' vision beyond the empirical to the transcendent.[112]

60

VII. Non-Christian religions and the religious needs of minority groups

Although the two themes of non-Christian religions and the needs of minority groups are related they are separate issues. It is not the presence of African, Asian, and Caribbean immigrants that forces us to recognize that religious education in Britain must not be limited to white Anglo-Saxon Protestantism. For years many pupils have asked for an introduction to other religions, and every opinion poll that has provided an opening for this sort of comment has shown that a significant proportion of the general public would like to see religious education in schools broadened in this way. The arrival of non-Christian religious groups in Britain reinforces a case that has already been argued on educational grounds.

1. Non-Christian religions

The society in which children are growing up today is an entirely new kind of society; the technological revolution has utterly transformed the world in which we live. We are frequently reminded that we now live in a global village in which we all know one another's business. In one hour a television programme can give an intelligent child the 'feel' of life in another country more effectively than the geography teacher of twenty years ago could do in half a term. It is now possible to introduce children to the religious experience of mankind in ways that were unheard of a generation ago. By the sensitive and imaginative use of audio-visual aids, pupils can be 'participant observers' in the daily life and the cultic acts of other lands and other times, and by such means they can sense something of the inner meaning as well as the outer form of other religions. This opens up new possibilities for work in schools.

The comparative study of religions was born at a time when the theory of evolution was dominant. Social historians and anthropologists would compare everything within range and then arrange beliefs and practices in a hierarchy ending with their own. This evolutionary view dominated the thinking of such pioneers as E. B. Tyler, Herbert Spencer, and James Frazer. Yet it was grossly unscientific, lighting on superficial resemblances and comparing things that are really very different. Unfortunately their views are still influencing popular thinking about other religions. Many young people are brought up to think of other religions and cultures as superstitious, irrational, and underdeveloped. This European frame of reference makes it difficult for pupils to enter into the religious experience of the rest of mankind or to appreciate the rich heritage and the present power of non-Christian religions.

The name 'Comparative Religion', which is widely used in schools, is itself misleading, since it implies both that religions can profitably be compared and that this is the main object of the exercise. We need a term, like 'the study of the world's religions', which leaves this question open. Attention is also now being paid to the many dimensions of each religion. In the past the focus of study has been too much on the doctrines of other religions and too little on the other five dimensions – mythology, ethical outlook, liturgical life, inner experience, and social expression. Each of these is a piece of the jigsaw puzzle, and for a true picture of a given religion all must be studied. Moreover, there are many academic standpoints from which they may be viewed; the insights of history, psychology, and sociology are particularly important. At the same time, every effort must be made to allow the phenomena to speak for themselves and not to impose upon them any presuppositions. The use of other disciplines is to facilitate understanding, not to explain things away. Religious beliefs and practices are not solely the product of non-religious factors.

In 1968 the University of Newcastle Institute of Education organized a conference to consider this aspect of religious education in schools and to take steps to facilitate its growth. The papers given at that conference have since been published under the title, *Comparative Religion in Education*,[113] and a group known as the Shap Working Party (named after the location of the conference) has carried forward this development, now on a national scale.[114] Many other parallel developments are taking place throughout the country. An inquiry as to the place of the comparative study of religion in one hundred West Riding schools may be fairly typical of the pattern elsewhere. The findings of the survey are worth quoting:

1 The subject is widely taught in schools in the West Riding, probably more than is generally realised, and is usually taken as part of RE. In view of the extent to which it is taught, and the desire for its expansion, it is a great pity that the subject is not given more attention in educational syllabuses. In the West Riding RE syllabus, for example, which is 132 pages long, only three-quarters of a page is given to this subject.

2 There is overwhelming support for the continued existence of the subject in the syllabus, and a considerable demand for its expansion. Any move-

62

ment to effect this expansion, however, must take into account the objections to the subject, which are mainly apologetic.

3 The comparative study of religion is thought by a large majority to be a subject suitable for all age groups. This must be taken into account in the preparation of suitable teaching material.

4 An even larger majority would like to see the subject incorporated into the examination system. It is regrettable, therefore, that more boards do not follow the example of the Northern and offer such an alternative . . .

5 The chief practical difficulties facing the subject are lack of books and suitable teaching aids, time and staff . . .

6 Perhaps the most striking feature of the respondents' answers was that the value of the comparative study of religions was seen in a much wider context than the RE lesson, in that its values were seen to be primarily the increase in tolerance and understanding, the widening of the pupil's horizons, as well as deepening his understanding of man and the world . . .[115]

2. Minority groups

When considering the religious needs of minority groups we have in mind first of all children who have a religious background that is not Christian; secondly children, including some immigrants, whose religious background is Christian but different from the usual pattern of English religion; and thirdly children from homes that explicitly reject all religion.

Immigrant children need to understand the religious heritage and the current religious outlook of the 'host' society as well as to understand the teaching and practice of their own faith. Similarly, if young people are to help to make the future, the 'hosts' need to understand and appreciate the culture, including the religious beliefs and practices, of their new neighbours. Religions play a much larger part in the personal, domestic, and social life of many immigrants than in the lives of most Englishmen. Where there are children of different religious traditions in the same class mutual understanding cannot be achieved if this dimension of life is ignored. The presence of members of different faiths should be welcomed as an asset in religious education, and in the dialogue between faiths local resources inside and outside the school should be used to the full. Sympathetic study of this kind will help to satisfy the immigrants' need for acceptance and for recognition of their cultural identity. It may also deepen the historical and cultural awareness of native English pupils.

It is not always realized that the separation of religion from general culture

63

is a comparatively modern Western device. In most countries of the world no such distinction is drawn. Many customs which seem purely secular to the Westerner are an important part of religion to an Indian or an African. The wearing of trousers by Muslim girls, the long hair and turbans of the Sikhs, and the observation of dietary rules by many minority groups are religious observances. Scores of other differences of custom arise directly or indirectly from differences of religion. Tolerance alone is not enough. Pupils belonging to minority faiths need to feel that their way of life is understood and its true worth appreciated.

The City of Birmingham was among the first to encounter the difficulties presented by the influx of large minority religious groups. A religious and cultural panel under the chairmanship of Professor John Hick of Birmingham University includes Sikhs, Muslims, Hindus, Jews, Catholics, and Protestants. We have already quoted (pp. 18–19) from their statement, in which they urge that religious education should provide a common background, with three elements, for all pupils:

a   Knowledge of Christianity
b   Elementary knowledge of the major world religions, especially those represented in the community
c   Moral education.

It is worth quoting further:

> In addition to this common background, and set within its context, we suggest that there should be opportunity within secondary education for more specialised religious study. We would suggest the following as the most suitable form for this to take.
>
> It would consist of a deeper and more particular study of one religion, normally the tradition to which the pupil adheres. In multi-religious schools this would be made possible by allowing . . . for options in part of the curriculum, the particular options that would be appropriate in a particular school depending upon the composition of its pupil body. There are schools in which two options would be appropriate (for example, Christianity and Judaism, or Christianity and Islam), and a few schools in which three or even four options would be called for.
>
> One might hope that the general educational value of a good syllabus of religious education would be such that heads would often wish to allocate three periods a week to it, in which case one of these three periods might suitably be devoted to this more particular study of one tradition.

We hope that it will also become possible for the CSE and GCE examinations in religious education to offer alternative papers corresponding to these options.

Most of the immigrant communities in Britain at the present time are liberal-minded and anxious to cooperate with Christians. If this cooperation is not welcomed attitudes may change and a great opportunity be lost. We believe that it should be possible to devise a framework for religious education in schools which is flexible enough to provide for the religious needs of minority groups as well as giving learning-skills and a common background to all. The needs of each religious group must be carefully assessed in its own right. Where the extra-curricular provisions seem adequate there may be little of a specific character for a school to add to the common background course, except to release pupils at certain times for their 'prescribed religious observances'. In other cases it may seem part of the duty of the school to see that these children receive some instruction from members of their own faith, when such teachers are available. We would resist, however, any suggestion that such instruction alone should be regarded as an adequate religious education. We believe that in a multi-racial and pluralistic society there must be dialogue between those holding different beliefs and growth in mutual understanding, not the widening of inherited divisions.

Reference was made earlier to the common European ignorance and prejudice against other religions and other cultures. Education can perform a service here by providing accurate, sympathetic information about the countries from which immigrants come – not only descriptive facts but the intentions, beliefs, and 'feel' of another culture. Appreciation is the key. For example, a number of leading artists and musicians have found inspiration in other cultures; Picasso and Modigliani have been affected by African art; Henry Moore was greatly influenced by the pre-Columbian work of the Amero-Indians. Yet nineteenth-century Europeans dismissed all this as the work of savages. The fertility of primitive imagination is now recognized.

There is a very great deal more to be discovered, both by teachers and pupils who are willing to suspend their own attitudes and enter into the feelings of those who say with pride, 'I am black!' 'I am a Jew!' 'I am a Jamaican!' 'I am a Pakistani!'

This approach is endorsed by the declaration on non-Christian religions promulgated by the second Vatican Council, 28 October 1965. Part of the text reads:

> The Catholic Church rejects nothing that is true and holy in these religions ... The Church therefore exhorts her sons, that through dialogue and

collaboration with the followers of other religions, carried out with prudence and love, and in witness to the Christian faith and life, they recognise, preserve and promote the good things, spiritual and moral, as well as the socio-cultural values found among these men.

It may be argued that some of the alternatives to religious faith, such as secular Humanism, Marxism, and Maoism deserve the same sympathetic study and attention. We would agree.

Research has shown repeatedly that what is taught and the methods used are much less important than the attitude of the teacher. Teachers' expectations of pupils are self-fulfilling. An informed, appreciative, and sympathetic teacher is best likely to meet the basic needs of pupils in any minority group.

This chapter has discussed the principles on which it seems to us, teaching should be based. We hope that many of the teaching units now being prepared will demonstrate how such teaching may be done. (See Chapter X, 'The project and its organization'.)

VIII. Religious education and moral education

Moral philosophers argue that the study of ethics and the study of religions are separate and distinct academic disciplines or areas of study. So, Atkinson:

> Morality, if autonomous, is equally distinct from and independent of science and religion – a position disappointing to those believers who want to subordinate morality to religion, to argue that it does not make sense to think of morality apart from religion, but encouraging to others who want rather to proceed to religion by way of morality.[116]

None the less, in schools in this country today, religious and moral education are widely regarded by pupil, parent, and teacher as interconnected. There is a general feeling that religious education (by which is usually meant the exposition of selected biblical passages, particularly those that contain the core of the Christian ethic) has as its principal educational aim the development of right moral attitudes in the pupil. An example of this thinking can be found in the Plowden Report where, under the general title, 'religious education', the following paragraph is introduced without the authors having first made any reference to the relationship between religion and morality:

> The school should be a community within which children should learn to live *the good life*. . . . By example at first hand children can learn to love and care for others, to be generous, kind and courageous. Good experiences in personal relationships in early life will make a most important contribution to an understanding of *spiritual and moral* values when children are older.[117]
> [Italics ours.]

There are a number of reasons why religious and moral education should be so linked in the minds of many educationists today. Some of these reasons have to do with the nature of the subjects themselves, and some, following from this, have to do with the history of education in this country.

Firstly, all of the great religions naturally prescribe for their adherents principles or codes for the ways of life they teach. Some of these prescriptions are more directly connected with the ritual or liturgical aspect of the religion than with the more specifically moral behaviour of the faithful – the offering of sacrifices, the observance of feast days, acts of communal and private prayer and worship. In the Christian religion this is sometimes described as the believer's 'duty towards God' and is an expression of what is always regarded as the first and great commandment – love towards God. But, in addition to these 'liturgical' prescriptions, all great religions require the believer to direct his present life in accordance with certain moral codes or principles. In this way the faith of the believer directly affects his moral behaviour towards other people in the community, within his family and in his own personal life. Hence no study of religion is complete if it does not examine the moral code or moral principles which form an important and essential part of each religion.

Secondly, religion and morality have many features in common. Each is concerned with attitudes and beliefs; each pronounces on right and wrong forms of behaviour. Thus a non-Christian might say of Jesus of Nazareth:

> His originality as a teacher lies partly in the permanent insight which continually he mediated in what he said, speaking relevantly and intelligently to the men and women whom he addressed, but repeatedly transcending their immediate situation, by any reckoning, enriching the moral understanding of those belonging to ages yet unknown.[118]

Thirdly, the religious belief of the majority of people in this country in the past has, as a matter of fact, had a direct and important effect upon the moral code which is enshrined in the law and is still widely accepted even by those with no specifically Christian belief. This is not to argue that morality should be thought of as subordinate to religion, nor that 'it does not make sense to think of morality apart from religion'. It is simply to state the fact that Christian ethical teaching lies at the core of Western morality and that this, in part, accounts for the link between moral and religious education in British schools.

Fourthly, it happens that the Christian Church has played a central role in the history and development of education in this country. This was discussed in the opening section of this working paper.

> In England, from the first, education was the creature of religion, the school was an adjunct of the Church, and the schoolmaster was an ecclesiastical officer.[119]

It is then not surprising that moral education in schools should for centuries have been taught in the context of the religious beliefs of the educators and that this legacy should remain with us today.

However, this close link between moral and religious education has led to reactions. There have been, and are today, sincere men and women who campaign for the rigid separation of moral and religious education, in some cases to the point of advocating the replacement of RE by 'ME'. As early as 1897 the Moral Instruction League was formed in an attempt to oust religious instruction given statutory recognition by the 1870 Elementary Education Act, and to replace it with a syllabus of ethical and moral teaching. The members of

68

this league were avowedly anti-religious and believed that a moral code could be developed from natural reason and human experience. The league was short-lived. Its chief mistake was, perhaps, to present moral education as an alternative to religious education instead of as a complement to it. It was really proposing another set of vested interests and prejudices in place of those it was attacking.

Educators whose primary interest is moral education and those whose primary interest is religious education still continue the debate, but, happily, the tendency to polarize these interests and to regard them as exclusive alternatives is less common. Many of those concerned with RE are fully aware that morality is an autonomous area of study, that religious perception and moral perception are as distinct as historical perception and aesthetic perception. Likewise, many whose interest is moral education recognize that the insights and accumulated wisdom of the great world religions cannot be ignored in any comprehensive scheme of moral education.

This attitude of mutual understanding and respect already promises to be more constructive and beneficial to the child than the former rivalry and antagonism. One example of such constructive cooperation was the publication of a joint statement by a group of Christians and Humanists based at the University of London Institute of Education. The following is an extract:

> We go on to ask whether there are any elements in the traditional approach to religious and moral education that are making the school's task even more difficult than it need be. Their attempts at moral education are sometimes vitiated by being so closely tied to religious education that at a later stage rejection of religion may well leave the adolescent without any moral foundation. But . . . we are not recommending that there should be in county schools two alternative courses, religious education and secular moral education, of which one or the other could be chosen by parents . . . The proposals outlined in this paper . . . involve a new approach at many points to the task of religious education in county schools, and also more definite planning for moral education, but each considered as closely related to the other.[120]

There are currently several projects – such as the Schools Council Moral Education Project and the Farmington Trust Research Unit [121] – engaged on research into moral education. We would like to contribute one further point to the discussion.

Attempts to take the moral teaching of a religion and to ignore the rest are bound to be unsatisfactory. Such moral teaching is part of an integral whole and is not the same if it is torn from its roots. For example, some have attempted to develop 'situation ethics' based on what 'love' dictates. This term 'love', however, can mean any one of a number of things. Those who appeal to it usually have in mind the Christian use, agape, described in St Paul's first letter to the Corinthians. In context it is part of a discussion of spiritual gifts granted to Christian believers. Out of context it loses its dynamic and its warrant. Many of the moral values which secular Humanists claim are drawn from 'the common pool of natural moral principles that all share' have really got into the pool from Christian springs. They would not be so taken for granted in a society untouched by Christianity.

Perhaps a comparative study of morals is required!

To sum up:

1 Moral knowledge is autonomous: it is perfectly possible to have moral education without reference to religious sanctions or presuppositions.

2 Schools should beware of linking morals too closely with one religious viewpoint, since some pupils who abandon that viewpoint may be left with no considered basis for morality. This applies particularly to voluntary aided schools and to independent schools having a religious foundation.

3 You cannot successfully take the moral code from a religion and leave the rest: the moral code of a religion is part of an organic whole; it is not the same thing when lifted out of its religious context.

4 There would still be a case for the study of religion in schools, even if it were not regarded as a fount of virtue.

5 If morals are not founded upon a religious view of life, they must have some adequate foundation; you cannot get far by an appeal to self-interest, or by appealing to a child as a rational moral being.

6 Although moral knowledge is mainly gained from experience, without explicit reference to religion, *ethical* religion adds a new dimension: wrong-doing is seen as having more than temporal significance; and, conversely, man's moral life is given an added dignity and significance if it matters to God.

7 There is no reason why moral education in school should be regarded as the responsibility of the RE department; much might be gained by a widespread recognition that this is a task for the whole school. When all departments contribute to this, it will be easier for the RE department to concentrate on its main task.

8 At the same time, whether in autonomous religious studies or in a course of integrated studies, the RE teacher has a special contribution to make to moral education, showing the links between moral problems, and moral concepts, and religious belief.

IX. Implications for teacher training[122]

When the 'open' educational approach to religious education has replaced the traditional 'confessional' teaching we believe that this subject will be a widely accepted and valued part of the curricula of maintained schools. It does, however, make enormous demands on the breadth of outlook and learning, the maturity of thought, and the sheer professional expertise of the teacher, and the success of this development will depend upon how far the colleges of education and the universities are able to produce teachers with the right sort of education to undertake it.

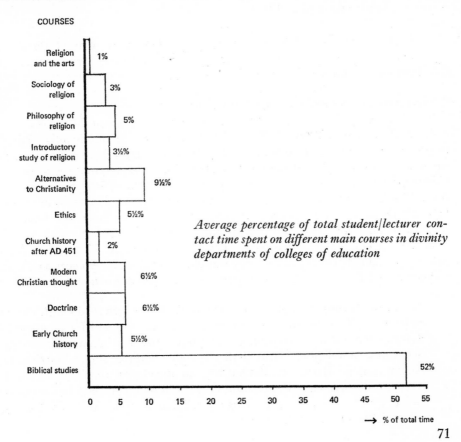

Average percentage of total student/lecturer contact time spent on different main courses in divinity departments of colleges of education

When the 1944 Education Act was first put into effect there was a serious shortage of trained teachers of religion, for the simple reason that until 1944 it could not be offered as a qualifying subject for the teacher's certificate. It became a common practice to depute this subject to anyone willing to take it, if he was dedicated to the faith and had a knowledge of the Bible. That inadequate view of the equipment required by an RE teacher is not uncommon today.

When the training colleges, (or colleges of education, as they are now called) began to organize main courses of study for RE teachers they were almost entirely biblical and doctrinal, sometimes with a little early Church history and, very occasionally, with a little philosophy of religion. This reproduced the pattern of training given to the tutors in the theology departments of the universities. It is interesting to note that an inquiry concerning the training of RE teachers in 1966 showed that main courses at colleges of education reached a good academic standard and that:

> 'syllabuses included Old Testament, New Testament, Church doctrine, philosophy of religion and in some cases New Testament Greek, and, in at least one, Hebrew.'[123]

The pattern had not really changed in twenty years.

The diagram (p. 71) shows the time given to different parts of the syllabuses in colleges of education today.[124] The syllabuses are still predominantly biblical (three colleges giving over 90 per cent of the time to this); other studies, though small, are more varied, and the most notable addition is 'alternatives to Christianity' which occupies second place, well ahead of 'doctrine', which comes third. There are, of course, considerable variations between colleges, but these figures indicate that the colleges are moving a little with the times, which is some cause for hope. This, however, is only a tiny first step.

In the universities the situation has been much the same. Until a few years ago the typical department of theology was almost exclusively preoccupied with orthodoxy and the Bible. As Smart describes one such department:

> ... all the theology taught in the Honours degree was to do with events and ideas before the end of the fifth century AD – except for a course in Reformation history. No sociology, no philosophy of religion, no comparative study of religion, no modern theology, nothing about Marxism or Humanism, no Barth, no Bonhoeffer, no Existential theology, no A. J. Ayer, no discussion of the relation between modern science and religious belief, nothing about the psychology of religion, no modern church history, no Christian ethics – need I go on?

He adds:

> . . . It has resulted in an over-intellectualist approach to religion as though it is a matter of doctrines and biblical revelation. It has not sufficiently induced in people a rich appreciation of the whole development of Christendom after the early centuries . . . It has failed to penetrate deeply into the nature of religious experience. It has left people rather ignorant of the wider world beyond the European tribe. It has left people unable to estimate Marxism or Humanism. It has said little about the role of religion in a contemporary culture. It has given people much of Hebrew history; much of Hellenistic theology. It has grounded people in the Bible. It has done good things; but it has neither obeyed the ordinary dictates of contemporary relevance . . . nor obeyed the logic of religious studies.[125]

Happily, in many universities this situation has been changing, although there is still a long way to go.

The teachers needed for the kind of work suggested by this working paper need to be people whose course of training has led them through subject areas which have brought them face to face with, and made them think deeply about, the response of man to his environment not only as this is expressed in his religion but as it is expressed in society, art, literature, philosophy, etc. The study of the works of great novelists, dramatists and poets, artists and philosophers, together with studies like history and sociology, can contribute to the education of such teachers as much as traditional 'religious' studies.

The study of the main religions of the world has an obvious educational justification in its own right, but the need for deeper understanding of the beliefs and customs of immigrant pupils may urge more concentration on one or two religions instead of a superficial world tour. Again, so long as most of the formal moral and social education is regarded as part of RE, teachers need some grounding in ethics and experience in handling controversial value questions in the classroom.

Sometimes the tutors say that their job is to interpret to their students what is done in university teaching and research. Fifty years ago this may have been a sound attitude, but it cannot safely be adopted today. The world is changing faster than most theological faculties. As teachers grow older they may feel like immigrants in a world that is going to be made by those who are now young. There is no sense in trying to get students to listen to problems which were burning issues when the tutor was younger and with which he still lives. Some theological faculties seem to go on with their traditional questions and problems. The meeting of world religions, the need for dialogue between them, has still

73

no significant place in many theological schools and seminaries. Tutors would be foolish to wait for a lead from such theological faculties rather than to take other steps to equip themselves and their students for the needs of today.

The time available in teacher training, whether in a three-year or a four-year course, is very limited. Obviously not all the subjects we have suggested can be fitted into every student-teacher's course. How can college and university departments cope? There are two answers to this: the first is provided by Smart:

> It is implicit in my argument that a person who is going to undertake the teaching of religious studies should have knowledge of at least three areas. First, he needs a grounding in his 'home' tradition; and this means in turn that he should be able to handle problems in understanding the biblical material; second, he needs grounding in the comparative study of religion – in the sense that his course should include an immersion in some traditions other than the 'home' tradition; third, he should be aware of modern developments in religious and atheistic thought and the sociology of religion. These three areas are interrelated . . . In brief, such a tripartite course will keep the student continually open to the methodological and philosophical problems surrounding the content with which he is working.[126]

The second answer comes from the recognition that education is concerned with teaching *how* rather than teaching *that*. Tutors are not textbooks but specialists in the art of learning. Their chief function is to teach their apprentices the skills of disciplined inquiry. Tutors should choose the *'representative ideas'* of a subject and select material and learning experiences to illustrate these. Like Confucius they should learn to give students one corner of a topic, but refuse to go on to the next until from the one they have discovered the other three corners.

They should also see that the *'distinctive methodologies'* of the discipline are followed until the students are familiar with those (hence Smart's reference, above, to the ability 'to handle problems in understanding the biblical material'). This is the real 'groundwork' of any subject, not the content – the ability to handle the tools and the raw materials of learning.

Notes and references

1 *Hansard*, Vol. CXCIX, col. 457, 1870.
2 Cited by S. J. Curtis in *A History of English Education from 1760* (University Tutorial Press, 1947), p. 277.
3 Cited by H. F. Matthews in his *Revolution in Religious Education* (Religious Education Press, 1966), p. 8.
4 See, for example, H. Loukes, *Teenage Religion* (SCM Press, 1961).
5 See, for example, J. W. D. Smith, *Religious Education in a Secular Setting* (SCM Press, 1969) and J. Donald, 'Fifteen years hard labour', *Bulletin* of the Association of Teachers of Religious Education in Scottish Secondary Schools, August 1970, pp. 8–12.
6 Quotations from *Religious Education*, November/December 1964 (Religious Education Association, New York).
7 *Moral and Religious Education in County Schools* (Social Morality Council, 1970), p. 12.
8 See, for example, C. Alves, *Religion and the Secondary School* (SCM Press, 1968); Gallup Poll, *Television and Religion* (ULP, 1964); R. J. Goldman, 'Do we want our children taught about God?', *New Society*, 27 May 1965; P. R. May, 'Why parents want religion in schools', *Learning for Living*, **6**, March 1967, 14–18; P. R. May, 'Why teachers want religion in schools', *Learning for Living*, **8**, September 1968, 13–17.
9 H. Loukes, *New Ground in Christian Education* (SCM Press, 1965), p. 94.
10 Ibid., p. 103.
11 Ibid., p. 130.
12 See I. T. Ramsey, *Religious Language* (SCM Press, 1957), pp. 17 ff.
13 See R. A. Spivey, 'Religion and public school education: a plan for the future', *A Journal of Church and State*, **X**, spring 1968, 193–205 (University of Florida).
14 See P. H. Hirst, 'Liberal education and the nature of knowledge', in R. D. Archambault (ed.), *Philosophical Analysis and Education* (Routledge, 1965), pp. 113–38.
15 *Report of the Consultative Committee of the Board of Education on Secondary Education with special reference to Grammar Schools and Technical High Schools* (HMSO, 1938), p. 208.
16 *15 to 18:* a report of the Central Advisory Council for Education (England) (HMSO, 1959), Vol. I, p. 44.
17 *Half our Future:* report of the Central Advisory Council for Education (England) (HMSO, 1963), p. 52.
18 Interim Statement submitted to Secretary of State for Education and Science, July 1969.

19 Ibid.

20 *Moral and Religious Education in County Schools* (Social Morality Council, 1970), p. 13.

21 *The Fourth R* (National Society and SPCK, 1970), p. 103.

22 See P. H. Phenix, *Education and the Worship of God* (Westminster Press, Philadelphia, 1966).

23 *The Guardian*, 14 September 1967.

24 P. H. Phenix, 'Religion in American public schools', in *Religion and Public Order* (University of Chicago Press, 1965), p. 87.

25 Ibid., pp. 87–8.

26 Ibid., pp. 90–1.

27 See, for example, J. Piaget, *The Child's Conception of the World* (Routledge, 1929) and R. J. Goldman, *Religious Thinking from Childhood to Adolescence* (Routledge, 1964).

28 *Children and their Primary Schools*: a report of the Central Advisory Council for Education (England) (HMSO, 1967), Vol. 1, p. 207, para. 572.

29 Phenix, 'Religion in American public schools', pp. 91–3.

30 Paper given to Board of Study in Divinity, University of Sussex School of Education, by Miss H. M. Adams, 1967.

31 *Committee on Higher Education:* report of Committee under the chairmanship of Lord Robbins, 1961–63 (HMSO, 1963).

32 Of more than two hundred publications listed at the end of the Durham Report, *The Fourth R*, all except ten appeared in the last ten years.

33 Much of the material for this chapter was prepared by D. J. Bates of Padgate College, Warrington.

34 *Half our Future:* a report of the Central Advisory Council for Education (England) (HMSO, 1963).

35 *Suggestions for Religious Education: West Riding Agreed Syllabus* (1966); *Religious Education in Wiltshire: an Agreed Syllabus of Religious Education* (1967); *Fullness of Life: an Exploration into Christian Faith for Primary Schools* and *Life and Worship: Agreed Syllabus of Religious Education, Senior Section* (Northants Education Committee, 1968); *Religion and Life: Agreed Syllabus* (Lancashire Education Committee, 1968); *Learning for Life: Agreed Syllabus* (Inner London Education Authority, 1968). See also *A Handbook of Thematic Material* (Kent Council of Religious Education, 1968).

36 See especially J. Piaget, *The Child's Conception of Number* (Routledge, 1952).

37 See R. J. Goldman, *Religious Thinking from Childhood to Adolescence* (Routledge, 1964) and R. J. Goldman, *Readiness for Religion* (Routledge, 1965).

38 R. J. Goldman, *Readiness for Religion* (Routledge, 1965), p. 49.

39 Ibid., p. 69.

40 Ibid., p. 197.

41 Ibid., p. 59.

42 Loc. cit.

43 See *Children and their Primary Schools*, Vol. 1, pp. 489–92.

44 Ibid., p. 207, para. 572.
45 Loc. cit.
46 *Half our Future*, p. 54, para. 163.
47 Ibid., p. 58, para. 174.
48 *Suggestions for Religious Education*, p. 3.
49 Ibid., p. 2.
50 See especially the articles on 'Religious education in a multi-racial community' and 'Moral education', pp. 23–5.
51 Ibid., p. 9.
52 Ibid., p. 36.
53 *Religious Education in Wiltshire*, pp. 98–102.
54 H. Loukes, *New Ground in Christian Education* (SCM Press, 1965), p. 98.
55 Ibid., p. 148.
56 Loc. cit.
57 Loc. cit.
58 Ibid., p. 158.
59 Ibid., p. 162.
60 Ibid., p. 175.
61 R. Acland, *We Teach them Wrong* (Gollancz, 1963).
62 R. Acland, *Curriculum or Life* (Gollancz, 1966).
63 Loukes, *New Ground in Christian Education*, p. 165.
64 Smart, *Secular Education and the Logic of Religion* (Faber, 1968), p. 90.
65 Ibid., p. 99.
66 Ibid., p. 97.
67 Ibid., p. 95.
68 Ibid., p. 99.
69 Ibid., pp. 105–6.
70 Ibid., p. 98.
71 Cox, *Changing Aims in Religious Education* (Routledge, 1966), p. 68.
72 E. Cox, 'Aims in RE', paper presented to London Society of Jews and Christians Conference, May 1970.
73 Cox, *Changing Aims in Religious Education*, p. 66.
74 K. E. Hyde, *Religious Learning in Adolescence* (Oliver & Boyd, 1965). Hyde found that learning in the secondary school is dependent upon a 'favourable' attitude towards the subject on the part of pupils.
75 Cox, *Changing Aims in Religious Education*, p. 89.
76 J. W. D. Smith, *Religious Education in a Secular Setting* (SCM Press, 1969).
77 Review circulated privately by School of Education, University of Birmingham.
78 Smith, *Religious Education in a Secular Setting*, p. 69.
79 Ibid., p. 22.
80 Ibid., p. 63. See also J. W. D. Smith's earlier writing on the psychology of religion, e.g. *Psychology and Religion in Early Childhood* (SCM Press, 1936).
81 J. W. D. Smith, letter, *Learning for Living*, **10**, September 1970, p. 30.
82 Smith, *Religious Education in a Secular Setting*, p. 85.

83 Ibid., p. 102.

84 Ibid., p. 101.

85 Ibid., p. 113.

86 J. W. D. Smith, letter, *Learning for Living*, **10**, September 1970, p. 30.

87 Even separation into denominational groups, as is now the practice, for example, in parts of Germany and in Ceylon, does not resolve this conflict of aims. It also reinforces religious barriers and does little to promote mutual understanding – one of the chief objectives of public education.

88 From a statement presented to the British Council of Churches by the British Humanist Association (March 1970).

89 Sten Rodhe, 'The teaching of religions', lecture given to Fifth Conference of Inter-European Commission on Church and School, July 1970.

90 Phenix, in *Religion and Public Order*, p. 108.

91 J. F. Kerr, *Changing the Curriculum* (ULP, 1968), p. 22.

92 See, for example, M. H. Duke, *Understanding the Adolescent* (SPCK, 1969); E. H. Erikson, *Identity: Youth and Crisis* (Faber, 1968); J. H. Hadfield, *Childhood and Adolescence* (Penguin, 1962); L. Hudson, *Contrary Imaginations: a Psychological Study of the English Schoolboy* (Methuen 1966 and Penguin); W. Kay, *Moral Development* (Allen & Unwin, 1968); K. Lovell, *Educational Psychology and Children* (ULP, 1958); E. A. Messer, *Children, Psychology and the Teacher* (McGraw-Hill, 1967); C. I. Sandström, *The Psychology of Childhood and Adolescence* (Penguin, 1966); W. D. Wall, *Adolescents in School and Society* (NFER, 1968).
See also: C. Alderson, *Magazines Teenagers Read* (Pergamon, 1968); M. De-la-Noy, *Young Once Only* (Epworth, 1965).

93 *Tonåringern och Livsfrågorna* (1969), reported by Sten Rodhe at Fifth Conference of Inter-European Commission on Church and School, July 1970.

94 See H. Loukes, *Teenage Religion* (SCM Press, 1961); K. E. Hyde, *Religious Learning in Adolescence* (Oliver & Boyd, 1965); C. Alves, *Religion and the Secondary School* (SCM Press, 1968), chapter 9.

95 See E. Cox, *Sixth Form Religion* (SCM Press, 1967); J. W. Daines, *Meaning or Muddle?* (University of Nottingham Institute of Education, 1966); R. J. Rees, *Background and Belief* (SCM Press, 1967).

96 N. Smart, *Secular Education and the Logic of Religion* (Faber, 1968), see especially pp. 13–20.

97 Ibid., pp. 13–14.

98 Ibid., pp. 15–18.

99 For a helpful discussion of this term, see J. Knox, *Myth and Truth* (Carey Kingsgate, 1966).

100 N. Smart, 'The comparative study of religion in schools', in C. Macy (ed.), *Let's Teach Them Right* (Pemberton, 1969), pp. 65–6.

101 For a full discussion of this theme from a theistic standpoint see P. H. Phenix, *Education and the Worship of God* (Westminster Press, Philadelphia, 1966).

102 *Raising the School Leaving Age: a Cooperative Programme of Research and Development*, Schools Council Working Paper 2, (HMSO, 1965); *Society and the Young School Leaver: a Humanities Programme in Preparation for the Raising of the School Leaving Age*, Schools Council Working Paper 11 (HMSO, 1967); *The Educational Implications of Social and Economic Change*, Schools Council Working Paper 12 (HMSO, 1967); *Community Service and the Curriculum*, Schools Council Working Paper 17 (HMSO, 1968); *The Middle Years of Schooling from 8 to 13*, Schools Council Working Paper 22 (HMSO, 1969); *General Studies 16–18*, Schools Council Working Paper 25 (Evans/Methuen Educational, 1969); *Humanities for the Young School Leaver: an Approach through Classics* (HMSO, 1967); *Humanities for the Young School Leaver: an Approach through English* (HMSO, 1968); *Humanities for the Young School Leaver: an Approach through History* (Evans/Methuen Educational, 1969); *Humanities for the Young School Leaver: an Approach through Religious Education* (Evans/Methuen Educational, 1969).

103 J. A. Comenius, *The Great Didactic* (1632), as quoted by M. Spinka (trans.), in *John Amos Comenius: that Incomparable Moravian* (Chicago University Press, 1942), p. 66.

104 C. P. Snow, *The Two Cultures and a Second Look* (Cambridge University Press, 1969), p. 14.

105 J. H. Plumb (ed.), *Crisis in the Humanities* (Penguin, 1964), p. 165.

106 A. N. Whitehead, *The Aims of Education* (Benn, 1932), p. 18.

107 Acland, *Curriculum or Life*, pp. 16 and 41.

108 *The Educational Implications of Social and Economic Change*, Schools Council Working Paper 12 (HMSO, 1967), pp. 81–3.

109 *Society and the Young School Leaver: a Humanities Programme in Preparation for the Raising of the School Leaving Age*, Schools Council Working Paper 11 (HMSO, 1967), paras 12–13.

110 Quoted by C. Alves, in his *Religion and the Secondary School* (SCM Press, 1968), p. 181.

111 *Humanities for the Young School Leaver: an Approach through Religious Education* (Evans/Methuen Educational, 1969), p. 14.

112 Ibid., p. 21.

113 J. R. Hinnells (ed.), *Comparative Religion in Education* (Oriel Press, Newcastle, 1969).

114 Secretaries: J. R. Hinnels (University of Manchester) and Peter Woodward, Borough Road College of Education, Isleworth, Middlesex (from whom details may be obtained).

115 For a full account of this survey see J. R. Hinnels (ed.), op. cit.

116 R. F. Atkinson, *Conduct: an Introduction to Moral Philosophy* (Macmillan, 1969), p. 107.

117 *Children and their Primary Schools:* a report of the Central Advisory Council for Education (England) (HMSO, 1967), Vol. 1, p. 206, para. 568.

118 D. M. Mackinnon in *Objections to Christian Belief* (Constable, 1963), p. 19.

119 A. F. Leach, *Education Charters and Documents* (CUP, 1911), p. xii.
120 *Religious and Moral Education* (Blackfriars Press, 1965), p. 3.
121 See J. Wilson, N. Williams, and B. Sugarman, *Introduction to Moral Education* (Penguin, 1967) and also N. Bull, *Moral Judgement from Childhood to Adolescence* (Routledge, 1969).
122 This is not strictly speaking in our 'brief' – but since the key to curriculum development is the quality and training of teachers some of the implications of our inquiry must be drawn. Others, like the British Council of Churches Working Party on the recruitment, training, and employment of teachers of RE, are looking into this more fully.
123 F. H. Hilliard, *Religious Education 1944–1984* (Allen & Unwin, 1966), p. 89.
124 Diagram adapted from D. Naylor, 'An enquiry into the content of college of education main course studies for the Certificate of Education' (MA research thesis, University of Lancaster, 1970, unpublished).
125 N. Smart, *Secular Education and the Logic of Religion* (Faber, 1968), pp. 101–3.
126 N. Smart in C. Macy (ed.), *Let's Teach them Right* (Pemberton, 1969), pp. 67–8.

Part II

Related issues

The main concern of this working paper has been to examine the character of religious education and from this to suggest an overall pattern for the future. Certain issues, however, are closely related and must be discussed, even though, in some instances, we do not wish at this stage to suggest final conclusions. We preface this discussion with some information about the project.

X. The project and its organization

The establishment of the Schools Council in 1964 was intended to give teachers a greater opportunity than ever before to shape the education of the future, and to provide an instrument whereby difficulties of long standing might be resolved. The Schools Council itself is a neutral body, and individual projects pursue their objectives freely and work out their practical implications. Although the Schools Council finances projects, the proposal to set up a particular project often comes from an outside body. This project was suggested by the Religious Studies Department of the University of Lancaster, in association with the Department of Educational Research. It is largely concerned with curriculum development. That is to say, its proposals are to be based not only on a survey of existing practice in, and literature on, religious education in schools, but on the contribution of the various educational disciplines to the theory and practice of teaching – philosophy, sociology, psychology, and history.

The staff of the Department of Religious Studies at Lancaster combine interest in traditional religious concerns (biblical studies and Christian theology) with other approaches whose value plus relevance to religious education are becoming more and more apparent (comparative study of religions, sociology of religion, and philosophy of religion). Professor Ninian Smart, Director of the Project and Head of Department, has already examined some of the theoretical issues in his *The Teacher and Christian Belief* and *Secular Education and the Logic of Religion*.[1]

The expressed aim of the project is:

> to evolve research and materials relevant to the construction of a satisfying programme of religious education in secondary schools, which takes into account the existence of voluntary schools and the presence of non-Christian populations in this country.

It is assumed that the teaching of the Christian religion will continue to be the dominant motif in religious education in this country, but that it should be possible to undertake this religious education in such a manner that it would be acceptable to people of differing convictions. The principles on which this might be done have been summarized as follows:

a   Insight should be given into the role of religion, and in particular the Christian religion, in the formation of British society.

83

b Insight should be given into the nature, challenge, and practical consequences of religious belief.

c Religious education should reckon with the actual pluralism of people and practice in contemporary British society and in the wider world.

d Religious education should be open, rather than dogmatic, and should require honesty of conviction, of whatever kind, in the teacher, without infringing the right to developed freedom of choice in the pupil.

e Religious education should be both relevant to the experience of the young and designed to broaden that experience towards an understanding of the religious dimension in human culture.

Work on the project began in September 1969, and it will continue for at least three years. In addition to the director, a deputy director was appointed from a college of education, three project officers with varied experience of teaching and allied work with children, and a full-time secretary.

The project is given advisory help by the permanent staff of the Schools Council and also by a consultative committee, set up specially for this purpose by the Council. Membership of this committee is drawn from a number of different parts of the country as well as from the university and the Schools Council itself, and includes a range of people from all relevant parts of the education service. The project is thus able to draw on a wide range of experience and expertise.

An initial period was spent surveying existing practice in secondary schools, current literature on religious education and previous research in this field. Links were established with those engaged on other Schools Council projects (for example, on programmes for primary schools, the middle years of schooling and neighbouring disciplines in secondary schools).

The questions raised by the various educational disciplines were discussed with specialists in these fields, both at the University of Lancaster and at other centres of learning, at home and abroad. These questions were also considered with a number of serving teachers. It is our conviction that a great deal of creative work is being done, and can be done, in schools. Over one hundred teachers, drawn from schools in and around the West Midlands, Lancashire, South-East London and the West Riding of Yorkshire, have been working with the project officers in the first stage of the work, and we hope to have the assistance of another fifty from three other areas in the second stage.

These teachers were not 'hand-picked' by the project. LEAs were asked to nominate a given number for a particular task. Beyond that no guidance was given as to their selection, although the hope was expressed that they would represent a variety of different types of school. A number of teachers from inde-

84

pendent schools were also co-opted, together with a few lecturers from colleges of education and university departments, an RE adviser and several others with specialist qualifications. The teachers thus represent a wide cross-section, not only of the different types of schools, county, voluntary, and independent, but the varied religious standpoints, Catholic and Protestant, Anglican and Free Church, conservative and liberal. There are also several representatives of non-Christian faiths. We have been encouraged to find that our efforts to carry with us all the main groups have been, so far as we can see, quite successful.

This dialogue between the different educational disciplines and between theory and practice has been stimulating and fruitful. As the real aims and objectives of religious education have become clear – and the principles which determine method and content, the teachers have been challenged to demonstrate how these might be put into practice. By working in groups and sub-groups a large number of experimental 'units of work' have been devised. These will be first tried out by their authors with their own classes, and then, after revision, by a number of other teachers. The results will be carefully evaluated, at both stages, and the units which seem best to illustrate the theoretical basis will be made available generally.

It is therefore hoped to produce an analysis of what, from an educational point of view, is feasible as the content of religious education in the total 11 to 16 age group, an outline syllabus covering the whole period from 11 to 16, and materials for specimen teaching units, with particular reference to:

a   Children who have just left primary school.
b   Young people who will finish school at 15 or 16 and not go on to further education.
c   Young people who will be carrying on beyond this age and who will very likely be faced with external examinations.
d   Children in areas where there are pressures arising from different religious beliefs.
e   Children who are below average in mental ability.

The variety of the units in course of preparation may be indicated by reference to a few of their titles:

The relevance of religious ideas to modern life
Nordic religion
Christ through many people's eyes
Islam and the Muslim way of life
Belief and Unbelief
Religion through culture – Judaism

Racial awareness
Mythology, religion, and science
How others see life
Social problems in a multi-racial society
Religious scriptures
Worship – Christian and pre-Christian.

As we wish to suggest a shift of emphasis in religious education teaching many of our initial teaching units will deal with new or less familiar topics. We hope that experience in using these will illustrate those principles which must be observed – and perhaps observed even more – when familiar traditional material is being studied.

XI. Probable lines of development

1 The project will recommend and illustrate an approach to religion in schools which is consonant with the approach to any other subject of study. This does not mean that it will be limited to a merely objective, scientific study of religion. There can be no true understanding of religion unless it transcends the informative.

2 Although, in the foreseeable future, the teaching of the Christian religion is bound to be the dominant motif in religious education in this country, in our work the subject will be given wider horizons to take account of the presence of non-Christian groups and to promote understanding and goodwill between people of varying religious convictions.

3 Children will be introduced to some of the living religions of the world at an earlier stage than hitherto. The approach will be largely thematic: the systematic examination of ideas will not be attempted until the final years of secondary schooling.

4 A much clearer distinction will be drawn between the role of the school in religious education and the role of the church, home, synagogue, or mosque.

5 Specific educational objectives will be carefully defined and will be used in the process of determining the content and methods of religious education.

6 Although in the lower forms attention will be paid to the common ground of religious education needed by all children ('Something to think about and something to think with' – Lancashire Agreed Syllabus) in the middle and upper forms there will be increasing opportunities for pupils to make a thorough study of one or more religions of their own choice.

7 While stressing the need for accurate information and the ability to reason clearly and logically about religious questions, greater attention will be paid to the role of the emotions in the formation of religious beliefs and attitudes. Specimen teaching units will, therefore, include the use of audio-visual materials, simulation exercises and drama, discovery by doing, and varied forms of expressive activity.

XII. Open-ended discussion: 'procedural neutrality'

Religious education, as we have defined it, is a process whereby ultimate questions are kept open, not a process of trying to close them. . . .
In practice the situation is not quite so simple. . . . The teacher cannot, in the end, be neutral, and he would be a poor teacher if he were. The pupil cannot, in the beginning be knowledgeable, or he would not be a pupil at all. In particular a teacher committed to a Christian position must find it difficult to deal, in a totally rational way, with declarations of atheism from boys and girls who are themselves merely repeating at second-hand what they have not understood for themselves.[2]

The . . . strategy . . . adopted by the project is to attempt to devise a method of teaching which should within itself guarantee that the teacher is doing all he can to protect people from his own bias, while advancing their understanding. This involves the teacher in a procedural neutrality in handling controversial issues. . . .[3]

Those quotations (the first from an earlier Schools Council publication, the second from the Director of the Schools Council/Nuffield Foundation Humanities Curriculum Project) raise certain questions: 1. What is 'open' teaching? and 2. What does it mean to be *procedurally* neutral?
One answer to the first question is provided by the report of the inquiry into religious education in secondary schools commissioned by the Education Department of the British Council of Churches. The official report is supplemented by a valuable commentary from Colin Alves, the secretary to the commission. In this book Alves sees religious education in schools as Christian education, with strong emphasis on its relation and relevance to the needs of the adolescent. He rejects the 'teaching about religion' approach as presenting religion

. . . in an emasculated form as a possibly interesting social or psychological phenomenon but not as a possible source of faith, power or truth.[4]

The schools, he argues, should be committed to a position of 'commendation' of Christianity, which is clearly the wish of the public and need not be 'closed' or dogmatic in character. So long as the official school position is 'open to chal-

88

lenge and discussion by the pupils'[5] and is officially recognized as such, there is nothing amiss, in Alves' view.

Can such an approach really be called open-ended? What is offered is not open-ended RE, but open-ended Christianity. J. W. D. Smith calls this 'an open-ended approach to a closed system of belief and practice'.[6]

Again, in what sense can a course of Christian education involving worship and the teaching of the scriptures, doctrines, and ethics of Christianity from infant school through to the end of secondary schooling with, at most, a grudging concession to non-Christian religions and non-religious viewpoints late in the secondary school, be considered 'open-ended'?

True openness, as we have pointed out earlier, involves an appreciative presentation of viable alternatives. Even with Alves' semi-detachment, the pupils will be in no doubt that the truth of Christianity is presupposed by the school. Such an atmosphere is scarcely conducive to a free and truly open approach, even to Christianity.

According to J. W. D. Smith, the questions which religious educationalists must increasingly face are:

> Must learning for living be done within the pattern of Christian belief and life? Is a truly 'open' approach really compatible with Christian education?[7]

We have given our answers to these questions in an earlier section of this working paper (Chapter II). The term 'procedural neutrality', however, raises another important issue. It was brought into currency by Lawrence Stenhouse, Director of the Schools Council/Nuffield Foundation Humanities Curriculum Project, now based at the University of East Anglia. This project has concentrated on the handling of controversial value questions in the classroom.

Stenhouse suggests, when confronted by such a question, that there are three possible answers. The first is for the school to 'attempt to transmit an agreed position adopted as a matter of policy'. This procedure is unacceptable for two reasons. Firstly, if the issue was controversial then it would be practically impossible for the school authorities to agree upon any one position. Secondly, even if it were possible to reach agreement within the school, to attempt to transmit one agreed position as a matter of policy would be to pretend that the issue was not, in fact, controversial.

The second course open to a school is to allow every teacher freely to give his own sincerely held point of view. Stenhouse suggests that there are two reasons why this cannot be the general rule. Firstly, the position of the teacher could quickly become impossible – what of the teacher who would advocate pre-marital sexual intercourse – a point of view which, though sincerely held, would be unlikely to gain parental approval? As a safeguard against such a situation it

F

would become necessary for interviewing panels to screen the moral beliefs and attitudes of candidates for the teaching profession in order to admit only those whose honestly held convictions were at all points socially acceptable. Secondly, Stenhouse suggests, many teachers are unaware of the strong authority-position they occupy in the classroom. An expression of opinion, which the teacher intends to be regarded as one opinion among many, is received by the pupils as apodictic law. Stenhouse adds:

> It is almost insuperably difficult for him [the teacher] to put forward his own points of view without implying that controversial issues can be settled on the basis of the authority of others.[8]

This discussion clears the way for the third and final possibility, the 'procedurally neutral' approach, wherein the teacher 'is doing all he can to protect pupils from his own bias, while advancing their understanding'. Stenhouse emphasizes that this role is not a negative one. It is 'a procedural neutrality in handling controversial issues which could be the basis of a professional ethic for dealing with controversy in the classroom'.

Three main objections to this view have been advanced. Firstly, it is objected that the role of the teacher is somehow impoverished, that this procedure makes him morally neuter rather than neutral. A teacher who is apparently unwilling to disclose his own moral point of view may be deemed by the child not to have one. This negative atmosphere within the classroom is unhealthy – far more so than in a class where the teacher advocates a point of view which can be vigorously attacked by the class.

Secondly, it is argued that a position of procedural neutrality is impossible. Even the most professional teacher's attitudes, prejudices, and beliefs colour his approach. Far better, it is said, for the teacher to bring out into the open his honest convictions, where they can be scrutinized and debated, than for him to declare no viewpoint but covertly, either intentionally or unintentionally, to direct the classroom discussion towards his own point of view.

Thirdly, it is argued, 'truth is not neutral':[9] teachers are mature adults, and the children have a right to expect them to have considered views on important controversial issues. It is perfectly possible for a teacher to present, with sincerity and reasoned argument, what he believes to be true and, at the same time, to respect his pupils' right and duty to do their own thinking. Both may be expressions of his love for his pupils.

The great merit of Stenhouse's views, and similar views expressed by John Wilson of the Farmington Trust Research Unit, is that they draw attention to the importance of seeing that children are in a position to make a balanced judgement on controversial issues, without the overbearing pressure of any person, whether

90

that person be admired or feared or held in some kind of awe. They also emphasize the fact that the teacher, whether he realizes it or not, is by virtue of his role a powerful figure of this sort. Stenhouse emphasizes that he is only urging *procedural* neutrality; when children are discussing controversial value questions they should be allowed to do their own thinking. The teacher should be an impartial chairman, seeing that all relevant viewpoints are fairly considered. This will include his own view, but he should arrange for this to be introduced as one among many opinions, put forward by someone else, perhaps from a book or a newspaper cutting.[10]

Whether or not this approach is adopted as part of a professional code for teachers, it is an approach which a teacher would do well to adopt for a few weeks. This will make him much more sensitive to the dialogue taking place between the pupils and the factors which help them to make informed decisions. It will also make him very conscious of the effect of every intervention he makes in the pupils' flow of conversation and thought. Education thrives on the airing of conflicting viewpoints in a common desire to let truth prevail. However, truth stands little chance of emerging from the conflict if one view is armed with a howitzer while the rest have only pea-shooters and catapults!

XIII. The Christian as R E teacher[11]

As some religions are 'missionary' faiths, teachers committed to them may feel that an impartial, undogmatic approach to religious education is inconsistent with their religious profession. This section, written from a Christian point of view, examines this issue. Similar considerations will apply in some measure to other faiths, and members of these religions may care to follow the argument with this in mind.

The Christian teacher has a responsibility both to teach and to witness. These two vocations may be related, but they are not identical. To illustrate the distinction between education and proclamation we may ask, 'How is the Christian faith communicated?', or 'How does a person become a Christian?' The answer, in one form or another, is that he becomes a Christian as a result of other Christians, i.e. as a result of some silent or vocal Christian witness. Christianity is knowledge communicated through Christian witness or proclamation. This may include the imparting of information, but it is not communicated by information alone. Witness may, of course, be silent, but where it is vocal we may term it proclamation. Within the context of the Church teaching is part of proclamation, but in the case of secular establishments this cannot be the case.

Education presupposes a common basis of agreement about what constitutes knowledge and what is only an opinion. At the present time Christianity, in the view of the majority, falls in the second category. The beliefs of Christians (and those of other faiths and ideologies) can only, in these conditions be presented as 'what some people believe'. We cannot present a religious belief as if all who do not accept it are knaves or fools. In brief, Christianity as truth no longer belongs to this common basis of agreement – except within the environment of the Church; it follows that outside this 'voluntary association' what Christians believe can only be classified as such, not as common knowledge shared by all.

The teacher who is a Christian will find himself involved in both education and proclamation – he is both a Christian *teacher* and a *Christian* teacher. The Christian is committed to witness all the time; the person who teaches and the person who proclaims is one and the same – there is no schizophrenia here. The two tasks are, however, distinct, though the distinction may not be immediately apparent. If we take the example of a Christian car salesman then the distinction between proclamation and his everyday task is easy to see. If a Christian car

92

salesman were to intrude his beliefs into his salesmanship, e.g. leaving a Gideon's Bible in the back seat of each car he sold, or putting Catholic Truth Society leaflets in log books, his efforts would probably be counter-productive. Yet his Christian faith may have some effect upon him and his work indirectly. Similarly, a Christian teacher of mathematics may herself sense God behind geometry – but she would not make that part of her geometry lesson. From here we may go on to ask where the Christian teacher of religious education stands. In a secular education system he must stand on the side of education; his task is to educate children. To sum up so far, there is a distinction between what a Christian is committed to doing on every possible occasion, i.e. the task of bearing witness to his faith, and his job or vocation which commits him to a certain restraint so as not to allow his convictions to intrude in ways that are inappropriate.

In speaking of education the Christian educator might argue that the child has a right to 'the best education possible'. He could go on to say that by this he means an education which would make children Christians. If by this he means that the child should be given understanding and insight into Christianity, and that this might result in commitment, such a statement is legitimate; but if the phrase is taken literally then there are both theological and educational objections which might be raised. From the point of view of theology one might quote the well-worn phrase that religion is 'caught not taught' – it is not something which is merely taught and learnt. From the educational angle the objection, if the aim is to make children Christians, is the familiar one of indoctrination; or, put more bluntly, that what is only opinion or belief is being taught as truth. This last statement describes what has all too often been the case in religious education. Such teaching is out of place in maintained schools in the present day, since the criterion of truth and knowledge by which we normally operate is the criterion of what is open to human reason and thus equally open to all. In religious conviction there is an element not open to human reason and rational investigation. A Christian would draw a distinction between rational knowledge and what is beyond merely rational inquiry. Religious conviction involves a response of the whole person, his feelings and will as well as intellect. Christianity must, therefore, be presented as 'what Christians believe', not 'what is the case'.

Should schools then concentrate on the *factual* knowledge – leaving the rest to the Church? Such a decision would be disastrous. What Christian believers say and do is meaningless if studied outside the Christian community of faith and practice. Religious language is only meaningful inside the religious community, i.e. we cannot present Christianity as straight, rational knowledge; the teacher must try to recreate the context in which religious language is meaningful. This task will stretch the imagination of both pupil and teacher to the full.

The difference between the approach suggested here and that which has, for example, been adopted in O- and A-level syllabuses in the past, and by the 1944 Education Act before them, should now be clear. The latter adopted an 'inside' position, assuming the truth of what was taught. In contrast, by emphasizing, for example, that in teaching the New Testament we are *listening* to witnesses, we are not prejudging the issue – although of course it should be recognized that some who hear this witness may decide to go along with it.

Little has been said of the role of the Church as an institution – we have correctly looked upon people as the Church. In conclusion, however, it is perhaps worth reiterating that what may be termed illegitimate in schools may be all right in the churches – here the presuppositions, chiefly that Christianity is true, are legitimate. Such presuppositions were previously shared by a majority in England but as this becomes less and less the case, Christians are obliged to take a much more open approach. In these changed circumstances it is a tragedy if Christians try to turn the clock back, or adopt an ostrich-like approach and fail to meet the challenge presented by contemporary society.

In the sphere of religious education the challenge is not to be met by Christian education which smuggles in Christian presuppositions, but rather by *religious* education which seeks to take the phenomenon of religion seriously and enables children to see what religion is all about. The freedom of the individual is then respected and the outcome of such an approach, supplemented by the silent witness of the teacher, may, in fact, lead to acceptance and commitment, but even if it leads to thoughtful and responsible rejection the education will have been worth while.

XIV. Religious education in voluntary aided and independent schools

This working paper has raised a number of questions about the nature of the subject called 'religious education' particularly as it is taught in county schools, where the rapid changes in society and the changed attitude towards religion are most marked.

In our society today children come into contact with various forms of Christianity and Humanism, and, in some areas, with other specific religious and quasi-religious viewpoints. Ignorance and prejudice against any religious group can do great harm. The object of the county school is not to induct children into a given religious viewpoint, but to promote sympathetic understanding of the religious groups around them, to encourage their personal quest for meaning and purpose, and to introduce them to the religious experience of mankind.

We have suggested that a clear dividing line needs to be drawn between attempts which adults make to get children to commit themselves to a religious viewpoint and attempts to get children to understand. The matter of commitment is the responsibility of the church, synagogue, mosque, family. In a pluralistic multi-belief society it cannot be the task of the maintained school.

Many church schools, of course, try to do both. The report of the 1969 DES seminar puts one side of the argument this way:

> Aided schools. . . may teach for commitment on the part of their pupils as well as for the personal enlightenment and enrichment which should characterize religious education in any school.[12]

Even here, however, it is important to recognize the distinction between these radically different objectives, if only to allow those whose parents wish it to ask for their children to be withdrawn from the former. Commitment is important, but it is not an integral part of education.

Some voluntary aided schools, and some independent schools with religious foundations, may feel that most of what we have written is not relevant to their situation. The school is an extension of the church, or synagogue, and what goes on in the parent body continues, without change of emphasis, in the school.

Many other such schools will find the issues raised in this working paper just as applicable to them as to county schools. Our impression is that most of the large boarding schools are aware that great changes have taken place in the climate of opinion about schools, and particularly about religion in schools. These changes have affected the outlook and attitudes of their pupils almost as much as those in county schools. Although parents, pupils, and staff agree that the school is supposed to be a religious community, for many the outward form is more religious than the inward reality.

We suggest that the same educational principles need to be observed by all schools, though in some schools the opportunities are greater. Religious foundations have made, and still do make, a unique contribution to the general field of education and to the spiritual welfare of society. They attempt to establish colonies in which religious education is woven into the full pattern of human life. They are in a unique position to ensure cooperation between the three agencies which loom largest in the lives of their children – home, school, and church – and carry the responsibility of seeing that these are turned outwards to participation and service in the wider world.

The role of the 'religious' school in society is not so clear today as it was fifty years ago, or perhaps even ten years ago. A recent article by Colin Alves discussed the role of the Church in society with special reference to her educational ministry.[13] He discussed the biblical symbols which have traditionally been used of the Church. In the early centuries she was regarded as the Ark, a God-given place of refuge from the storms of destruction round about. After the time of Constantine she became the husbandman tilling the field of the world, or the shepherd guiding and directing society. Sometimes the world was pictured as a boat, and the Church its helmsman, commissioned to steer it safe into harbour. Today, however, three other symbols have come to the fore, each suggesting a more humble role for the Church in society. One is the symbol of leaven, working within the dough. The second is the symbol of the servant, caring for and watching over the best interests of mankind. The third is the symbol of salt, the cleanser, the primitive antiseptic, protecting the body of society from disease and decay.

These current symbols of the Church are perhaps clues to the role of the Church in education today and to the task of the 'religious' school in relation to its pupils.

XV. Worship and the school assembly

The requirements of the 1944 Education Act on worship sought to regularize the existing practice of school assembly in the majority of schools, but laid down no specific guidelines as to how this should be tackled. The criticisms which have followed may now be seen to fall mainly into two categories: attacks on theory and reactions to what actually happens in practice.

Many of the objections to the very idea of having the secular school involved in an act of worship are voiced by informed educationists who have strong religious convictions of their own, as well as by secularists within the profession of teaching at school, college, and university level. There seems also to be a growing surge of dissent among some older pupils.

Practice varies enormously between schools, and seems to depend on a number of variables which include the district no less than the attitudes of head teachers and staff. School tradition may seek to impose the dead but respectable air of a nineteenth-century Church Office, or it may permit experiments which allow infinite variety and material from many sources.

A good deal of honest thinking and hard appraisal has been going on during the past decade, with some courageous and costly experiments in schools not governed by the 1944 Act, so that any future legislators on this subject will need to look at both the maintained and the independent sectors of education in order to get a fully informed and contemporary picture.

Some confusion has undoubtedly arisen because of the administrative convenience which combines with the school's act of worship the routine chores of an assembly, resulting all too often in the much parodied 'hymn sandwich with football results', which does justice to neither element. On the other hand, the sacred–secular sandwich is supported by some who are concerned at the ease with which worship can become separated from life, with disastrous effects on the understanding of both. They therefore integrate the routine chores with the worship, and regard this as an expression of an important principle.

Those who wish to see the religious element omitted point to the absurdity and dishonesty of expecting pupils from a wide variety of backgrounds to participate in something that the majority of their parents have little time for, and which they cannot yet evaluate objectively, however they react now. There are also fears that non-conforming staff may miss promotion.

Educational arguments in favour speak of the need for a quiet period in adolescence, the fostering of school spirit, the inculcation of values and the promotion of social awareness, and the civic advantage of having some acquaintance with ritual. There are also those who feel that experience of worship is a necessary adjunct to religious education, among other subjects.

Any analysis of practical objections to assembly–worship soon reveals that inaudible or unintelligible readings, hymns at the wrong pitch with indefensibly dreadful words, boredom, irrelevance, and professional incompetence (or lack of interest) vie with physical discomforts due to timing, lack of seating, inadequate ventilation, and other unnecessary hazards.

There is little doubt that the administrative burden of preparing an imaginative act of assembly–worship for every day of the school year is beyond the resources of all but the most talented and dedicated head teachers or those to whom they delegate – and public poverty in this field affects the professional image, and is often taken by visitors to reflect the morale of the school.

This picture can be modified where assembly–worship is given a priority by the foundation of the school and the interest of the staff: there are large secondary schools with comfortable seating for all pupils, audio-visual media of professional standards, and a ration of time, money, and prestige which brings every department of the school into the planning and production during the year's scheme.

But if the majority of schools are to continue with worship any practical suggestions, staff training or equipment allowances, will have to be complemented by a renewed *raison d'être* that will overcome the increasingly hostile reaction of those staff and pupils who feel that the present arrangements are an impertinent waste of their time and the educational resources of the nation.

The report of the DES seminar on religious education held in March 1969, speaks of the views of the seminar's members on worship in schools in the following paragraph:

> Though worship is an experience in which pupils should have the opportunity to share, the corporate act of worship in secondary schools is often a stumbling block; it is extremely difficult to provide a significant personal, or even communal, experience for an entire school, and not only members of staff but many pupils are today either indifferent or hostile to it. Formality and dullness are the major causes, rather than the nature of worship itself; probably the first essential is to provide variety in worship and to offer to groups of staff and pupils the opportunity for genuine planning and participation. Many assemblies are too large and their purpose unclear, but some schools have already demonstrated that it is possible to design

assemblies which appear useful and credible to humanist and secular staff and pupils as well as to Christians. In such schools the assembly is not always religious (in the narrow sense) in tone and content; over a period it provides an exchange of philosophies and approaches to life, and the Christian and the humanist alike add to their knowledge of each other's beliefs and practices. Such a spirit of dialogue can greatly enrich a school. Many recently published agreed syllabuses offer excellent suggestions on all these topics and on the diverse resources available to the teacher. A major need is for widespread study and discussion of these syllabuses.[14]

Obviously the multi-religious situation that exists in many schools calls for a general reconsideration of the aims and purposes of the school assembly. Most immigrant pupils attend morning worship, although there is some apprehension about this on the part of parents. If they find that the assembly is concerned almost exclusively with the propagation of Christian beliefs then more immigrant parents will want to press their legal rights of withdrawal.

In some situations withdrawal, of a limited and specific kind, may have its place. For example, in some areas Muslim children are now permitted to use the school hall on Friday afternoon to say their prayers under the guidance of the local Imam. This has reduced absenteeism from school on Fridays, and it has helped to create an atmosphere of trust between Muslim parents and the school. It has also brought native English children into direct contact with the practices of another religion.[15]

Withdrawal itself, however, ought not to be regarded as the most satisfactory solution to the problem. Changes in the form of the school assembly must spring directly from the needs of the situation, but the object should be to devise a form that is relevant to all the members of the community. This is not to encourage the holding of hybrid, multi-faith services, which imply a unity of intention which is not there and distort the material used by lifting it right out of its proper context. That is a way to confuse, not to promote inter-faith understanding.

However, there are ways in which the assembly can be used from time to time to impart some understanding of other religions. For example, some schools mark the principal festivals and red letter days of religious groups within the community by inviting members of those groups to plan a special celebration in which all can participate, if only as observers, in the religious life of the group. There is something to be said for this. Christians have a good deal to learn about worship in its widest aspects from Asians whose religion embraces a much wider area of life than that of most Christians. Religious attitudes, social customs, art, music, and dance are all expressions of worship.

In some situations there is value in finding ways in which immigrant children can share, on occasion, certain aspects of their religious beliefs and practices with the school as a whole – so long as it is remembered that full understanding is only possible when these are seen in the context of the believing community and the home.

School worship in secondary schools is often formalized, arid, and removed from every other aspect of life. The occasional introduction of the music, drama, dance, and religious literature of another culture may be one way of breaking with this sterile convention. It may even lead to a rediscovery of forgotten dimensions of Christian worship – particularly if the school contains West Indian or Cypriot Christian children.

The 'brief' of the present project made no mention of the school assembly, but clearly it has a bearing on our work and must be taken into account. This is part of the legacy from the early days of universal education, and it reflects the practice of church schools and an age when daily prayer was a common practice in the home. It has survived and been adapted by several generations, but recently with less success, especially in secondary schools. Nevertheless, it still has a strong hold, especially in primary schools. It is significant that the MacKay Report,[16] which in effect advocated the abolition of RE in the schools of Ontario, recommended the continuance of the daily worship in primary schools. This aspect of the curriculum really requires a curriculum development project of its own![17]

XVI. External examinations and religious education

The function of an examination is to measure reliably the degree to which the objectives of a course of study have been achieved. The curriculum planning process passes through a number of stages, the first of which is the selection of aims, goals, and objectives and the last of which is evaluation or assessment (part of which may be internal or external examinations). Examinations should be seen as an integral part of the curriculum, related directly to the content of the course, which in turn arises directly from the aims and objectives decided at the outset. It follows from this that those concerned with curriculum development must consider from the start what evaluation methods – formal examinations, continuous assessment, reports on topic work, etc. – are most likely to measure reliably the effectiveness of the course of studies. This needs to be said because external examination results are used for a number of external purposes, and examinations are sometimes planned with little regard to the real aims and objectives of the schools. Where this happens there is a tendency for the examination to dictate the content of the course of study rather than the other way round, and the whole process of responsible curriculum planning is 'stood on its head'.

Examinations have been justified variously as having the function of encouraging (or goading) pupils and teachers to work; as a method of selecting students for further study, potential teachers and employees for other occupations, and as instruments to preserve, or to change, existing curricula.[18]

It is, of course, right that those planning a system of public examinations should consider its likely effect on the curriculum as a whole. It is equally appropriate that employers and those selecting students for higher education should take examination results into account. Similarly, there is little doubt that the prospect of an external examination is one way of encouraging academic rigour in a course of study.

At the same time, when these incidental effects of examinations override their true purpose it is understandable that teachers should feel frustrated and complain that examinations distort the curriculum, compelling them to neglect important aspects of the learning process and, because of the limited time, to concentrate on those most easily examinable.

Teachers of religious education sometimes make this complaint. They also complain that, where pupils are required – for entrance to a profession or a higher education course – to gain five passes at GCE O-level, many will choose a course of religious knowledge, not because of the merits or interest of the subject, but because, at the examinable level, it is regarded as an 'easy option'. This attitude further restricts the scope of the teacher.

To sum up so far: education is primarily concerned with the development of certain cognitive skills, attitudes, and interests – 'changes in pupil behaviour which it is intended to bring about by learning'. The acquisition of accurate factual information is important, but it is only one measure of the success of the course. Unless external examinations pay full regard to the educational objectives of a course of study, the content and the methods of study will be examination oriented instead of being true to the nature of the subject and the needs of the pupils.

One question which vexes teachers of the 'humanities' is whether the attainment of some of the declared objectives of such courses can be measured by formal examinations. In religious education, for example, it is relatively straight-forward to devise tests of the pupil's factual knowledge of religious texts, beliefs, doctrines, and practices. It is even fairly easy to test a pupil's ability to compare differing beliefs, to trace development in thought and to understand the implications of certain parables or myths for people today. But is it possible to measure reliably those objectives which seek to encourage 'sympathetic understanding', 'tolerant attitudes', and 'insights into'?

Some educationists believe that it is not. So McIntyre and Wainwright:

> It is justifiable to teach in such a way that pupils will be encouraged to consider where they stand in relation to issues raised, and so that they will be likely to acquire such socially constructive attitudes as tolerance and concern for social justice. Yet it would be quite inappropriate to set an examination which gave credit to pupils with an 'approved' set of beliefs and attitudes. Apart from considerations of morality, it is almost impossible to construct an attitude test on which faking cannot be achieved by those determined to do so.[19]

While not everyone would agree that examinations are worse than useless in the affective realm, few would dispute that the problems of constructing a reliable test are many and weighty. Some would argue that examinations which require cognitive skills in religious education are valuable in so far as a thorough knowledge of the facts of religious beliefs and practices is a necessary prerequisite for 'sympathetic appreciation of' and 'insights into' those beliefs and practices.

102

So J. K. Scobbie, from a Scottish viewpoint:

> One would expect that a high proportion of the material in an RK (cert.) examination would be factual and objective.[20]

He adds elsewhere:

> . . . it is worthwhile pointing out that the lack of specialist students of religion in our secondary schools may be illustrated by the profound ignorance of religion revealed when this subject is debated and discussed in the classroom or in school societies. Senior pupils who might be considered intellectually mature in many other fields express notions of religion no further developed than those acquired in the primary classes of the Sunday school. . . If even a few of the pupils had studied RK (cert.) to fourth or fifth year level, there would be some chance of the debate on religion rising above childish conceptions.[21]

But if we allow that the greater part of the examination should be concerned with factual knowledge, we are left with the problem mentioned at the beginning of this chapter; namely, that with the knowledge that matters of fact *about* religion will be the main requirement of examinations, the pupil and the teacher will tend to give this aspect of the course more emphasis than what many consider to be of equal, if not more, importance: the quality of insight into and understanding of religious belief and practice. McIntyre and Wainwright put the case thus:

> It is not sufficient that the achievement of some of the objectives of Religious Education can be assessed by examinations; it is also necessary that these should be the dominant objectives. If this is not the case, then not only do examination results give a distorted impression of the effectiveness of the course as a whole, but much worse, the examination in practice distorts the objectives of the course itself.[22]

From this, it should be clear that any attempt to devise an examination syllabus in religious education must be undertaken in full knowledge of the fact that, if the course is to be examined then the attainment of *all* the declared objectives must be reliably measured.[23] If this is not done, then the content of the course will almost certainly suffer in consequence.

Notes and references

1 N. Smart, *The Teacher and Christian Belief* (James Clarke, 1964) and *Secular Education and the Logic of Religion* (Faber, 1968).
2 *Humanities for the Young School Leaver: an Approach through Religious Education* (Evans/Methuen Educational, 1969), p. 32.
3 L. Stenhouse, 'Controversial value issues in the classroom', in W. G. Carr (ed.), *Values and the Curriculum: a Report of the Fourth International Curriculum Conference* (National Education Association, Washington, 1970), p. 106.
4 C. Alves, *Religion and the Secondary School* (SCM Press, 1968), p. 148.
5 Ibid., p. 186.
6 J. W. D. Smith, *Religious Education in a Secular Setting* (SCM Press, 1969), p. 101.
7 Ibid., p. 69.
8 Quotations from Stenhouse, op. cit., p. 106.
9 See M. V. C. Jeffreys, *Truth is not Neutral* (Religious Education Press, 1969).
10 For a discussion of the difficulties involved in this approach see B. G. Mitchell, 'Indoctrination' in *The Fourth R* (National Society and SPCK, 1970). See especially his summary of Burke's argument, pp. 357–8.
11 Summary of a lecture 'Education and/or proclamation' by Rev. R. C. Morgan, lecturer in New Testament studies, University of Lancaster, April 1969.
12 DES, 'Religious education: present and future', *Reports on Education*, No. 58, September 1969.
13 C. Alves, 'Religious education and the role of the church in society', *Faith and Unity*, **XIV**, January 1970, 4–7.
14 DES, op. cit., p. 3.
15 *Religious Education in a Multi-Religious Society* (British Council of Churches and Community Relations Commission, 1969).
16 *Religious Information and Moral Development* (Ontario Department of Education, 1969).
17 A good starting-point would be the article by Dr John Hull on 'Worship and the curriculum', *Journal of Curriculum Studies*, **1**, November 1969, 208–19.
18 See, for example, some of the arguments advanced in support of the proposed Q- and F-level examinations in *Proposals for the Curriculum and Examinations in the Sixth Form: a joint Statement* (Schools Council and SCUE, 1969).
19 D. McIntyre and A. Wainwright in *Curriculum and Examinations in Religious Education* (Oliver & Boyd, 1968), p. 19.
20 J. K. Scobbie in *Curriculum and Examinations*, p. 9.
21 Ibid., pp. 7–8.
22 McIntyre and Wainwright, op. cit., p. 19.
23 One interesting attempt at this links teaching, mainly by interdisciplinary inquiry, with a CSE Mode III examination by continuous assessment. (Details from W. F. Clarke, St Helier Boys' Secondary School, Jersey.)